Justification of Cyber Harassment Among Turkish Youths

I0125235

Seda Gökçe Turan

Justification of Cyber Harassment Among Turkish Youths

PETER LANG

Lausanne • Berlin • Bruxelles • Chennai • New York • Oxford

Library of Congress Cataloging-in-Publication Data
A CIP catalog record for this book has been applied for at the
Library of Congress.

Bibliographic information published by the
Deutsche Nationalbibliothek
The German National Library lists this publication in the German National
Bibliography; detailed bibliographic data is available on the Internet at
http://dnb.d-nb.de.

The cover image courtesy Krakenimages / shutterstock.com

ISBN 978-3-631-89210-7 (Print)
E-ISBN 978-3-631-89357-9 (E-PDF)
E-ISBN 978-3-631-89358-6 (E-PUB)
10.3726/b20392

© 2023 Peter Lang Group AG, Lausanne
Published by Peter Lang GmbH, Berlin, Deutschland

info@peterlang.com - www.peterlang.com

All rights reserved.
All parts of this publication are protected by copyright.
Any utilisation outside the strict limits of the copyright law, without the
permission of the publisher, is forbidden and liable to prosecution.
This applies in particular to reproductions, translations, microfilming, and
storage and processing in electronic retrieval systems.

This publication has been peer reviewed.

Again…
To whom that inspire me from my childhood…

PREFACE

It is obvious that violence is multilayer phenomenon. Much of the research focus of reasons of violence, reasons of violence and how could we prevent violence. For the 21st century those concerns become vary and the most important one is justification of violence. If people commit a violence and get punishment about this, it could be lead to rehabilitation. But, if people think the victim is "deserve" violence, violence is "normal" and desensation toward violence acts, the rehabilitation seems impossible.

In this study, which is developed from my PhD thesis, I aim to understand the basic question: How people justify cyber-violence? I hope this study will help to clarify this concept, make people aware to how justification of cyber-violence effect the cyber-violence rate and block the rehabilitation options.

Seda Gökçe Turan
İstanbul, 2022

CONTENTS

INTRODUCTION

The issue of violence and the media and their effect on individuals are important phenomenon in media theories and research. The phenomenon of violence, which can be triggered or normalized by the interaction between the individual and society, is examined and discussed not only in the media context but also in many other disciplines in terms of different variables. Although, there is not a single factor that affect the phenomenon of violence; developments and improvements in media tools and technology have now caused violence to be discussed in different dimensions.

In this book, justification of cyberbullying will be analyzed in depth in terms of social media usage, cyber-harassment and emotional deafness (alexithymia), which are among the factors that will cause individuals to perceive violence as legitimate through communication tools, on individuals' perception of violence as a legitimate is discussed. For the second part of the book the research that conducted at Turkey with university students will be presented.

Considering the opinions in the literature that situations such as excessive internet use and excessive time spending in social media cause social isolation of individuals, the relationship between emotional deafness and exposure to violence in the media and seeing violence as justified has aroused curiosity. Normalizing violence and seeing it as a legitimate right are two concepts that have blur line. Excessive exposure to any stimulus, especially in the media, can lead to desensitization and emotional deafness. But there will of course be a difference between normalizing a phenomenon and seeing it as a legitimate right. It is thought that the fact that individuals in society see it as a right rather than being desensitized to the phenomenon of violence will pose a danger not only for the sociological structure but also for the justice system.

The phenomenon of violence in the media has been examined in a wide range from movies, characters in series, behaviors, violence in video games to pornography, harassment and rape in the internet environment. In this book, the phenomenon of media and violence was evaluated within the framework of gaining legitimacy in the context of cyber-violence and alexithymia (emotional deafness) among Turkish Youths' and the effect of information literacy on this.

The conceptual and theoretical part of the research is divided into two parts. In the light of the studies conducted in the literature, the effect of media and technology on individuals is mentioned in the second part of the conceptual part of the research. This effect can be positive as well as related to how violence in the media drives individuals' behavior in the long term. In this context, deindividualization effect, belief-in-a-just-world concept and "General Aggression Model" were evaluated as a guide in terms of examining how violence in the media shapes individuals and society in general.

In the last part of the conceptual part, it is tried to reveal the effect of violence on the alexitimia (emotional deafness) and legitimization of cyber-violence in new media, how individuals become desensitize in the intense bombardment of violence and how they perceive cyber-violence as a legitimate right and at the same time justify it.

In the second part of the book the research that conducted with Turkish University Students (400 students) will presented.

PART I

1. DIGITAL MEDIA LITERACY

This century the most significant characteristic is that post-truth era of alternative facts. People not always could be aware what information real and what is fake. So, media researchers stress about the importance of digital media literacy. The concept of digital media literacy (DML) is defined in the literature as the ability to access, analyze, create and use digital media. This includes everything from knowing how to find credible information online to being able to communicate using digitally mediated technologies (Hague and Payton, 2010, cited in Mrah, 2022: 176). According to Mrah (2022) through digital media literacy instruction, not only students but also individuals will be better placed to use digital technology to engage in self-directed enquiry and to discriminate between multiple sources of information.

Lv (2022) evaluated the concept of digital media literacy in terms of digital virtual technology. According to Lv (2022) digital virtual technology with media survival as an important representation, with the rapid development of the new media technology represented by the internet, digital virtual technology with its entertainment, personalized service, open sharing of content, form of real-time interaction and other characteristics strongly attract the young group. In the digital virtual era, teenagers' digital media literacy has not only become one of the essential qualities for them to cope with global competition, but also an essential quality for college students to realize lifelong learning (p. 1). Suwana (2021) noted that digital media literacy is critical for everyone, everywhere, in the modern era to develop, as digital media literacy skills help internet users to be not only consumers of online information but also active digital citizens. Moreover, Suwana (2021) explained digital media literacy skills with traditional media literacy skills. Media literacy is considered a set of reading skills based on critical thinking. However, scholars have been refining the definition of media literacy for more than a decade in the light of technological development.

As we said before, this era is so appropriate for manipulating individuals and society. So, we have to develop some "weapons" for protecting our children and youths. Moreover, not only children and youths but also elderly people and adults are under risk of digital media manipulation. In addition, the book's subject of "justification of cyber-harassment" could be very dangerous lack of digital media literacy skills. We should give importance to not only for children but also youths' digital media literacy skills. With the state of this idea Tekoniemi, Kotilainen, Maasiltaand Lempiainen (2022) underlined the importance of digital media literacy. They noted that disinformation spread over the digital social networks has been identified as a threat to democracies, economy, and to individuals. Threats such as fake news or conspiracy theories grasp communication and democracy and infect them with suspicion. Fake news, disinformation or information that spread with new technologies such as deepfake are seen as new challenges and risks. They not only spread the disinformation but also lead to justification of cyber-violence or natural violence. So, as researchers argued digital media literacy seems the most effective weapon for combatting with this issue.

Before explaining the relationship between justification in depth we should explain relationship between media and violence.

2. RELATIONSHIP BETWEEN MEDIA AND VIOLENCE

The presentation of violence in the media, the intense and continuous exposure of individuals to violence have effects on people not only in the social and communication dimension but also in psychological and neurological aspects. In this part of the study, the relationship between media and violence will be discussed in the context of social media and social networks, the effect of media on individuals and violence.

2.1. Social Media, Social Networks and Communication

According to Christie and Dill (2016), computer centered communication and its function is remained unclear. Especially at the point where digital media products and information technology tools reach, every individual can reach the information they want, regardless of their social status or geographical location; access and access to information has changed not only what individuals know, but also how they know what they know (Flanagin and Metzger, 2008). Similarly, the rapid accessibility of information from different sources and on a very large scale has made the authenticity, quality and accuracy of the information questionable (Flanagin and Metzger, 2008). McKenna and Bargh (2000) have stated that the internet alone will not cause anything, so researchers' social identity, social interaction and relationship-building skills will be different from real life on the internet.

Many theories about the internet consider the internet to be a means of social transformation. New communication tools and the internet permeate all areas of individuals' lives and assume a mediating role in the change of concepts and values (Gürel and Yakin, 2007). The presence of different profiles and identities on the internet is seen as evidence of the democratic structure of the internet (George, 2006). Not only the effect on the structure of society, but also the conflict between generations in the age of "digital technology," the effect of information technology tools in many areas such as political discourses and methods of communication is seen, so much so that young generations are considered as the generation that is "washed with bitlets and bytes" from birth (Jones and Czerniewicz, 2010). In parallel with the increase in the place of individuals in their daily lives in social and economic terms, the internet, whose importance, speed and usage area are also increasing. It is a structure that includes traditional communication tools such as watching television, reading newspapers and listening to the radio. Social media (Facebook, Twitter, YouTube, LinkedIn, etc.) in this structure are seen as a freer environment by users and individuals express themselves more easily (İnceoğlu and Çoban, 2015). However, Gürel and Yakın (2007), who examined the website that shows the participatory dictionary feature containing the comments of the authors named Ekşi Sözlük, state that there is an extremely intense hierarchy and control mechanism in the operation and structuring of this site through the example of Ekşi Sözlük. From the point of view of children and young people, information technology tools (telephone, computer, videos, video games, cyber networks, etc.) play a central role in their daily lives (Huesmann, 2007: S6). Due to many social and cultural differences, social media has become an important area where adolescents come together and socialize informally with their peers. Boyd (2014: 5) defines this informal environment as "networked publics." Merwe (2013) discussed the psychological impact of the use of information technology tools on adolescents within the framework of information literacy and online social behavior. As a result of the research, Merwe (2013) stated that communication with peers has a great impact on the social and behavioral processes of adolescents. In the context of the research conducted by Yardi and Boyd (2010) to evaluate the polarization between groups on Twitter, 30,000 tweets were examined. According to the homogeneity theory, Yardi and Boyd (2010) stated that individuals are mostly in groups where they feel closer to them, and that the opposite is observed on Twitter, and that individuals are in complex and opposite groups or are exposed to such messages / tweets. In the George Tiller case (the murder of a doctor who performed a late-term abortion), it was found that like-minded people responded more to each other, and that group identity was stronger, but there was more dissociation among different-minded individuals.

Boyd (2014) discussed internet use among adolescents by comparing it with their experiences in their teenage years. Boyd (2014) sees the internet as an "escape mechanism" because he feels inadequate in social relationships. However, when we look at today's young people, adolescents' participation in the virtual environment is not a strange or unusual situation, but on the contrary, it is normal or even expected. In addition, Boyd (2014) described social media sites such as Facebook, Twitter, and Instagram as "cool" environments, and stated that adolescents think that they do not really exist when they are not on these sites.

According to Croteau and Hoynes (2000), through the developments and improvements in electronic media, the old roles and social identities of individuals are blurred or reshaped. In addition, the dominant information reaching individuals, especially with television, removes barriers between individuals and changes old patterns in communication (Croteau and Hoynes, 2000). Karagülle and Çaycı (2014) stated that social networks will enrich the social life of individuals as long as they do not replace face-to-face communication, but when they take precedence over real-world communication and social life, the life of the individual is limited to a digital environment and digital communication. In addition, although social networks are considered as easier communication channels due to time constraints in modern society, it has been an undeniable fact that they make the individual passive (Karagülle and Çaycı, 2014).

Ögel (2012) argued about the impact of the internet on social structure from different perspectives. According to him, other technologies have also affected human life, but the internet has changed the entire social structure, creating changes in human nature along with the social structure. Ögel (2012) also stated the relationship between the internet and the media, that the internet is as usable as all kinds of media, but the difference is that the internet is democratic and social. Ögel even called the internet "the beginning of a new era."

In terms of adolescents' social lives, students who show depressive disorder and feel lonely use the internet more and chat with people both familiar and unfamiliar. Adolescents stated that this situation was good for their social loneliness and reduced the feeling of loneliness (Ybarra et al., 2005). In addition, it has been stated by researchers that communication in a digital environment, where identity is not clear, can turn into a socially supportive environment for adolescents if used carefully (Varnhagen, 2007).

Merwe (2013) categorized the reason adolescents prefer digital communication rather than face-to-face communication as follows: Invisibility, asynchronousness, thinking just like a play, and the idea that everyone is equal. In addition, Merwe (2013), who departed from the definitions made by Suler (2004), examined the personality characteristics of adolescents in the digital environment; psychopathic, narcissistic, schizoid, paranoid, depressed, manic, masochistic, obsessive-compulsive, hysterical and schizotypal. When invisibility or anonymity from user characteristics is examined on the basis of Social Identity Theory, it allows individuals to behave more aggressively and aggressively to those who are against their own views and increases the tendency of individuals to these behaviors.

With the rapid development of communication technologies and the fact that the internet is one of the vital elements of daily life, differences have started to emerge in the communication process. It is not possible for the mass media to give "simultaneous" feedback because consumers are passively positioned. However, with the digitalization of mass media, simultaneous mutual communication has become possible. Individuals can simultaneously conduct face-to-face communication with communication mediated by a machine. In other words, while an individual is communicating with a person who is next to him, he may be communicating with another individual through digital communication technology at the same time (Şener, 2016).

Madianou and Miller (2012) adopted an approach called "Polymedia" to examine the consequences of digital media in interpersonal communication. In this approach, the researchers evaluated how users used new media as a means of communication instead of an abstract technology environment in which their profiles were catalogued. Polymedia's main concern is the social, emotional and moral ground of every personal media tool. For example, the means chosen for communicating were more preferred in previous periods than the telephone or the letter, because in long distance communication, these two tools were both cheaper and more easily accessible. In other words, the reason for using the communication tool and browsing in multiple internet environments are related to the experience and management of interpersonal relationships. Polymedia is not only interested in the use of technology alone, but also in the relationship between sociality and technology. There are many different opinions and explanations that have been put forward about the use of the internet and information technologies by individuals. Subrahmanyam and Greenfield (2008) stated that adolescents use communication and information technology to strengthen their social friendship relationships, but as time goes by, they close themselves to their own digital world and maintain their friendships from here, from the digital environment.

It is clear that there is a segment of adolescents who use the internet not only to advance and consolidate their existing friendship, but also to talk and meet romantic relationships and strangers. Just like friendship relationships, romantic relationships are one of the most important features of adolescence. Adolescents use electronic media and mobile phones to consolidate their romantic relationships (Mason, 2008). Teenage Research Unlimited (2007) found that almost 1/4 of teens in a relationship communicate with their girlfriend or boyfriend between midnight and 5 a.m. using a cell phone or text message.

In the information age, not only about the use of the internet, but also about the mobile phone, the different motivations of mobile phone use have been tried to be revealed. For example, Bal (2013) studied 1,175 students attending university and found their motivation for cell phone use; fashion/status, functionality/socialization, fun/relaxation, mobility and information. When the results on the basis of gender are examined, it is seen that women talk and text more using their mobile phones than men; It has been determined that men attach more importance to features such as the 3-G feature of the mobile phone and the possibility of gaming.

Studies on the use of social media in Turkey and adolescents' perspective on this issue will be examined and awareness on this issue will be tried to be revealed.

Yılmaz et al. (2015) examined social media and participation behaviors within the framework of the concept of digital activism and found that the participants gave intensive support to activist activities in virtual environments as a result of the study they carried out with the data collected by the surveys applied to 260 university students in the virtual environment. For the participants, e-mail, social media and signature campaigns are considered as a means of expressing people's reactions. In particular, the awareness of online signature campaigns and the high participation in these campaigns are other results of the research. Based on this, researchers see self-expression as clictivists as part of the solution to the problem instead of traditionally supporting activism movements. Yılmaz et al. (2015) interpreted the findings of the research as digital activism behavior is seen more intensely because the digital environment allows interaction, allows individuals to express their ideas easily, participate in discussions with different people or groups and even organize.

As a result of his research that the game called "Smeet" played in social media discusses how individuals change the reality phenomenon, Sucu (2012) stated that when users observe their dialogues while playing games, the game becomes a place to communicate, and players attach a meaning to this game as a "communicative meeting place."

Gökçearslan and Günbatar (2012) conducted a study with 172 students in Bursa in order to examine the internet addiction levels of high school students and the factors affecting this level (gender, parents' education status, personal computer ownership, duration of using social networks). As a result of the research, 2.33 % of the participants were identified as internet addicted and 4.65 % were identified as in the risk group. While male students scored higher in terms of internet addiction than female students, it was found that students who used the internet for more than 3 hours on a daily basis showed more addictive behavior.

Akça and Başer (2011) stated that not only social media but also developing technology shapes privacy and privacy. According to Akça and Başer (2011), who discussed the activities of eavesdropping and secret surveillance over the tape scandals during the 2011 Turkish general elections, they argued that in a theoretical context, the legal rules governing the eavesdropping and the secret monitoring of people's private information and private lives are not reassuring and that this issue is an issue that can only be resolved by technical methods.

In his study in which Satan (2011) discussed the studies on new media and socialization in the literature, he listed the most important motivations that enable people to use social media sites as social escape, information, interaction and entertainment.

Göker et al. (2010) determined that students use Facebook intensively as a result of the research they conducted with 486 participants to determine the Facebook usage habits of university students. Participants who were previously members of Facebook but canceled their membership as the reason for cancelation; harassment, accessibility to everyone, deviation from purpose and loss of time. While 71.9 % of the participants stated that not all of their friends on the Facebook page were from their social circles, 82.9 % stated that they did not share all of their personal information on the Facebook page. Participants at most (40.6 %) liked Facebook's ability to help find old (57.2 %), thought Facebook reinforced friendships in social life, and 40.6 % believed that Facebook did not help communicate with the opposite sex.

Gürel and Yalın (2007) examine and discuss the interactive database named Ekşi Sözlük and define Ekşi Sözlük as "a virtual formation that mediates the questioning of the patterns of what is true and operates on the basis of spontaneous order" (p: 203).

When the studies conducted abroad are examined, it is revealed that a connection has been established between social media sites and interpersonal relationships.

Christie and Dill (2016) examined the impact of anonymity in cyberspace on their approach to people who may or may not oppose their views in a study they conducted with 256 participants.

Stephens et al. (2016) examined 80,923 tweets about road fights in traffic over a 13-month period, and found that, on average, 2 out of 3 tweets contained resentment toward the other driver and stated that the other driver had behaved inappropriately. The most frequently thrown tweets are those related to drivers speeding. The most commonly used judgments about other drivers were summarized as "idiot," "incompetent" and "should not drive."

Clayton (2014) conducted a study of 581 active Twitter users aged 18–67 to investigate how Twitter use affects interpersonal relationships and romantic relationships and found that active Twitter use leads to discord between couples in an unhappy relationship, resulting in betrayal, separation and divorce in the future.

DreBing et al. (2014) conducted an online survey to examine "stalking" behaviors and their effects on people in cyberspace and social media sites, and they conducted a survey with 6,379 people. Participants actively use the German social media site "StudiVZ." While the behavior of following in the virtual environment was determined as 6.3 %, it was revealed that these behaviors were related to real life. In other words, people follow the relationships of their ex-lovers in the virtual environment. While virtual tracking is predominantly carried out by men, the victims are mostly women. Compared to people who were not exposed to virtual follow-up, it was found that people who were exposed to virtual follow-up were less psychologically healthy.

Valenzuela et al. (2014) as a result of their research to examine the relationship between the use of social media sites, marital satisfaction and divorce rates in America, there is a negative relationship between social media use and marital satisfaction and happiness; they found that there was a positive relationship between the problems in the relationship and thinking about the divorce. In addition, the increase in the divorce rate with the increase in the use of Facebook between 2008 and 2010 in the United States is one of the striking results of the research.

Barak et al. (2008) examined the studies conducted in the literature based on the thesis that online groups have a positive effect on individuals because they provide the opportunity to express themselves, especially in stressful events, and methodologically, it would be difficult to measure the empowering effect of online groups on individuals without considering other factors, but nevertheless, when the studies were examined, online groups would be psychologically effective on individuals after stressful events. empowering, positive effect will be mentioned.

3. EFFECTS OF MEDIA ON INDIVIDUALS

Rapid developments in technology, science and communication in the world have caused radical changes in different dimensions of social life and these developments have not only changed the perception of time and space of individuals, but also changed the established perceptions and definitions (Önk and Selçuk, 2014). Many researchers have evaluated the effects of traditional media and new media on individuals and societies with different perspectives and disciplines. In this part of the study, the findings in the literature will be tried to be presented.

Zorlu (2016) states that it is widely accepted that modeling and identifying with the characters reflected in the media affects the learning processes of children, young people and even adults, while Huesmann (2007: S6) argued that mass media have an impact on the values, beliefs, thoughts and behaviors of children and young people, albeit positively or negatively. Benedikter and Fitz (2011) stated that the use, development and spread of technology took place very quickly, especially social media stood out as an indispensable element in the lives of individuals, but they suggested that the benefits of social media and technology have now reached the dimension of "technophilia" (Technology admiration). However, unlike this argument, Steinerman et al. (2013) stated that when combined with the desire for social participation of technophilia, people are more inclined to participate as participants in scientific studies such as research and experiments. Brown (2002: 42) examined the mass media in terms of the sexual development of adolescents and evaluated adolescents as a field where they learn sexuality rather than just seeing it, and more importantly, stated that through mass media, adolescents form their own attitudes and beliefs about sexuality. According to Croteau and Hoynes (2000), who evaluate the role of the media in the social relations of individuals from a sociological perspective, the media has assumed a vital role in many parts of daily life. The impact of the media on individuals is not limited to the known, but much more than media messages can affect individuals. Media also influences how individuals learn about the world and interact with each other. That is, the media is connected with the process of social relations (Ceoteau and Hoynes). Tutar (2012) stated that in a social structure that can be called an information society, mass media is one of the factors that play a role in the formation of the attitudes of individuals and the reinforcement of these attitudes. Dönmez (2003) stated that for many in society, television is the constant "bad guy" who can be blamed for every problem of American society.

In addition to sexuality, individualization and social effects, the fact that children are influenced by cartoons and play deadly games rather than the media affecting children with violent elements especially in cartoons attracts the attention of researchers. From the point of view of our country, it is quite thought-provoking that he was influenced by the cartoon called Pokemon that he watched in Mersin and likened himself to one of the flying heroes in the cartoon, jumped from his house on the 7th floor to fly and died, and that a 12-year-old boy in Adana wanted to fly with the rope he tied to the fan on the ceiling in his house by emulating the film called Spider-Man, and unfortunately lost his life as a result of the rope wrapping around his neck.

In addition to traditional media, some pathological (diseased) situations can be seen in the use of social media also. For example, a pathological state of admiration can also be observed, unlike just innocently admiring a series or a famous artist. Admiration, which is pathological, can be defined in two ways: obsessively following anyone on social media and acting wearily. Similarly, pathological admiration can manifest itself within groups and these people can pave the way for violence, alienation and cult behaviors in the media to become widespread (Jenson and Lewis, 1992). Pathological admirations that were discussed through television programs and artists in the 1990s continue to increase with the effect of the internet and social media today. Gans (2014) on media and pathology presents a different kind of discussion. According to Gans (2014), it is not possible to attribute a long-term, lasting impact to any content offered by the media or to a media medium. However, it seems likely to have negative effects on media addicts, whose entire lives are shaped only around the media in cognitive and emotional dimensions, considering the pathological conditions of individuals. In addition to all this, Gans (2014) does not ignore the fact that the media has an impact on all segments of society.

The perception of reality and the effect of the media on children and adolescents are also prominent issues in literature research. According to the findings, it was tried to reveal the perception levels of children and adolescents about whether the visuals they are exposed to in the media are fiction or reality. Cantor and Riddle (2014) found that as children age, they are more affected by the real "dangerous" images they see in the media and less affected by fantastic images. Children who are much younger in age are more afraid of impossible items (spaces, monsters, etc.) that are not possible to be real, with the effect of developmental characteristics.

İnceoğlu and Akıner (2008) focuses on the problem of "representation of the child in the media" in the context of children, the media and violence. According to her, children are often presented in the media as victims of war, poverty and exploitation, as well as being manipulated in competition programs, and in programs that are concerned about ratings or tragedy, they are tools for emotional exploitation. Moreover, a wide variety of views have been put forward regarding the effects of the media on individuals. According to Şirin (2006), instead of making a distinction between good and bad for the media, it is more appropriate to separate the purpose of use of individuals as good or bad. Aydoğan and Büyükyılmaz (2017) argues that the media in general instills ideological ideas, entertainment, empty satisfactions and narcissistic feelings in individuals instead of providing individuals with information and enlightenment. Ulaş et al. (2012) stated that individuals who are against authority through the media experience a secret sense of satisfaction when they see the humiliation of authoritarian figures through the media, that individuals empathize with the people shown in the media and have the chance to see the mistakes of others, and that the media also offers individuals models that they can imitate. Güven (2015) directly intervenes in the public perception through news programs with the way the media conveys the events and at the same time it can direct and manage social tastes and perception with the entertainment programs it produces.

There are five types of influence of the media on the individual. Behavioral impact if a media receiver performs certain behaviors presented by media messages; attitudinal impact if messages shape the recipient's beliefs and values; cognitive impact if messages shape the recipient's thoughts; emotional impact if the messages affect the recipient's emotions such as anxiety, enthusiasm, joy, sadness; If changes occur in the arousal and other physical reactions of the receivers with media messages, physical effects can be mentioned (Ulaş et al., 2012).

Now, it's time to turn findings conducted in Turkey on the effects of the media on individuals.

Narmanlıoğlu (2016) touched upon the differences between the reality presented on television and the real world in which they live and conducted research with the focus group method with foreign graduate students in Turkey in order to compare the images about Turkey and the Turkish people with the social life on the channels broadcasting in Turkey and discussed the results within the framework of "sowing theory." According to the results of the research, there are differences between the participants' television experiences and what they observe in the real world. According to the participants, especially in the series, the codes of male-female relations and social interaction give an image of an open society; however, in the social environment in which the participants live, the interactions are more about privacy. In television news, there is much more violence than in the real world of experiences and observations according to the participants.

Unlike the negative effects of the media on individuals and society, when it is considered that the media is the mirror of the society, it is seen that the violent incidents in the society are increasingly reflected in the media. According to the results of Teyfur's (2014) study by examining violent news between 1998 and 2004 in order to investigate how news about violence in schools was reflected in various newspapers; While the violence applied by teachers to students was at the forefront in the content of the news reflected in the press between March 1, 1998 and March 1, 1999, it was seen that between March 1, 2003 and March 1, 2004, students and parents as well as teachers were the subject of violence in the content of the news. Within the scope of the research, it was seen that the news of harassment, which is an important problem not only in schools but also in society, increased from 5.97 % between 1998 and 1999 to 9.15 % between 2003 and 2004. Again, when the comparison was made between periods, it was found that the news about stabbing incidents in schools increased from 1.49 % to 4.23 % and the news about drug use increased from 4.48 % to 10.56 %.

Çebi (2013) in his article discussing the functions and effects of the media based on the French sociologist Tarde's Model of Public Space, stated that the media has a functional, effect on individuals and societies and that this effect is effective even in the construction of the nation state, nation and law.

While findings on the effects of traditional media on individuals continued, studies on the effects of social media on an individual basis began to be carried out with the creation and spread of Facebook in 2004. While studies on social media are shaped around questions such as "Is social media a tool, a place, a content or a type of communication?," the rapid evolution of digital technology emerges as a challenge for researchers (Şener, 2016).

Gencer (2012) examined ATV, Kanal D and Show TV with the content analysis method in a 5-day period to evaluate the agenda-setting process of the media and investigated the opinions of university students about the effect of media on agenda formation. As a result of the research; A significant relationship was found between the agenda of the students and the agenda presented by the mass media. According to Gencer (2012), the issues that constitute the agendas of the students evaluated within the scope of the research do not emerge spontaneously but are formed with the information conveyed through mass media.

Şeker and Şimşek (2012) conducted an in-depth interview with 15 high school students to investigate the impact of the television series Magnificent Century on high school students. As a result of their study, the students' comments such as "I cooled off from Kanuni after the series" and "My admiration for Kanuni decreased" and the fact that they defined the series as "shameful," "distorted historical facts" and "unfair to Turkish history" were found remarkable by the researchers.

Kara (2011) conducted a study with 435 people in Manisa to investigate the effect of visual media on family members. According to the results of the research; While 70.35 % of the participants think that television series negatively affect child psychology, the rate of those who think that marriage programs disrupt general morality is 42.82 %. In the research, 68.96 % of the participants stated that television has a negative effect on intra-family communication, 82.76 % that visual media sets the agenda, 85.06 % that media has a great power over society, and 66.66 % that visual media creates awareness in society.

There are so many other findings that conducted at abroad. Now it's time to examine them.

Cranwell et al. (2016) conducted a study of 1,094 adolescents aged 11–17 to examine the relationship between tobacco and alcohol consumption in UK video games and the prevalence of tobacco and alcohol consumption among young people and found that adolescents exposed to tobacco and alcohol consumption in popular video games were more likely to use tobacco and alcohol.

Cheng et al. (2016) conducted an online survey with 2047 participants after the earthquake and tsunami disaster in Japan in 2011 to examine in depth how mass media and social media affect individuals' perceptions after disasters and their behavior after disasters. As a result of this research based on the sowing theory, Cheng et al. (2016) found that mass media, especially television, affected people who did not directly experience the disaster more, while social media had more repercussions on people directly affected by the disaster. Establishing a positive bond between families and society and the media; It was found to be very effective in terms of accelerating civilian communication, taking more altruistic actions and taking measures for possible disasters in the future.

Fox and Vendemia (2016) evaluated the effects of social media on users by examining people's self-reflection on social media sites and their behavior of comparing photos with other users. With 1,686 participants, the behaviors of men and women including situations where they feel bad or good by posting photos, editing photos and comparing them with others' photos on social media sites were examined within the scope of the study. As a result of the research, some differences in gender were identified. According to this, women organize more photos than men and feel worse than men when compared. Body image and the tendency to physically compare themselves play a role as a mediating effect in these results.

4. VIOLENCE

In the Turkish Dictionary of the Turkish Language Association, the word violence is defined as "The degree of a movement, a power; tendentiousness, harshness, extremism in emotion and behavior, reconciliation of those who hold opposing views, use of brute force instead of persuasion."

In times when there were no social rules, where there was no social and social structure to ensure the safety of the person, and when information and information exchange were very limited, "aggressive" behavior was one of the characteristics that helped human survival the most (Savrun, 2000). However, today, violence and aggression are not accepted due to social rules. Basically, it is possible to group violence into four classes. Playful violence has been defined as violence that is not diseased, does not aim at destruction or hatred, and is more often caused by an effort to demonstrate its prowess. An example of this type of violence is the war games of primitive tribes. In reactive violence, it is the type of violence that a person resorts to protect his own or others' life, freedom, honor and property. Religious violence is a more advanced dimension of reactive violence and is related to both reactive violence and shows a pathological (diseased) pattern. In reactive violence, the aim is to protect from the danger of harm, while in vindictive violence, harm has already been done, and therefore violence has no defensive function. Balancing violence has been defined as violence that replaces productivity in a powerless person (Erdal and Erdal, 2012).

According to Köknel (2000), there are many natural, physical and spiritual causes of individual and social violence, as well as interaction between these causes. But more importantly, people have seen the aggression that originated from them as right and justified with different defense mechanisms throughout history, in other words, they have legitimized violence. Yazıcı (2013) stated that violence exists with different causes and dimensions, and that although a type of violence is common in some societies, it is noteworthy that it is seen as exceptional or not at all in some societies; explained this situation with the sociological differences experienced by societies in the process of change from traditional to modern, from modern to post-modern and the effect of these differences on individuals.

In the literature, it is seen that the concepts of violence and aggression/aggressive behavior are used together. Aggression/aggressive behavior is defined as any deliberately harmful, disturbing behavior (Bushman and Huesmann, 2012). There are three main characteristics in aggressive behavior. The first is that aggressive behaviors are behaviors that can be observed from the outside. For example, behaviors in which a person hits, uses verbal violence, shouts, hits, etc. are behaviors that can be seen from the outside. Aggressive behavior is not just feelings such as resentment, anger or thoughts such as "the desire to kill someone." It is also worth noting that there are behaviors that take place between at least two people, since aggressive behaviors can be seen by others. Second, aggressive behavior is intentional. Accidental or accidental behavior is not considered aggressive behavior. For example, aggressive behavior such as a drunk driver hitting anyone is not considered aggressive behavior. Third, the person who is subjected to aggressive behavior should not want to be harmed. In other words, suicide and masochistic behaviors are not within the scope of aggressive behavior. Because in suicide, there is no such thing as the individual avoiding harm, while masochistic individuals also enjoy pain (Bushman and Huesmann, 2012).

Perception is the subject of research in cognitive sciences and includes how individuals make sense of existing events in their minds, interpret them and react within this framework (Köknel, 2000). Since perception is a phenomenon that varies from person to person and from society to society, the studies carried out are guiding in this regard.

Deveci et al. (2008) conducted research with 110 primary school fifth grade students in order to examine the perceptions of violence of primary school students; fighting, beating, mistreating, swearing, yelling, hurting. Similarly, children stated that the most frequent violent incidents they encountered were beatings, fights, snatching, extortion and theft. While the children spoke to pre-vent violence and offered suggestions such as agreement, love, respect, tolerance, peace, complaining to the police, education, punishing, calm, separating those who fight, they expressed their feelings about violence with words such as "I feel sad, I am afraid, I feel very bad, I want to take revenge, I get excited, I put myself in its place, I get angry, I pity, I cry, I hate, I feel ashamed."

Hargrave (2003) conducted a study on how adolescents aged 9–13 interpret screen violence. As a result of the research, it was revealed that the participants were able to distinguish between fictional violence and real violence, as well as to make evaluations about the "justifiable" use of violence, and this evaluation affected their perception of violent visuals. The most important finding of the research is that there was no combination between fictitious violence and real violence in the minds of the participants. According to Hargrave (2003), chil-dren create a "library" for themselves with the violent images they see on tele-vision or in movies, and their reactions to violent images are shaped by age, gender, maturity and individual circumstances.

4.1. Nature of Violence

Violence is not a phenomenon that only related with individuals. It is a multi-layer phenomenon related with personal characteristics and society characteristics. For violence behaviors, problem-solving skills and cognitive schemas could be evaluated together. According to Calvete (2008) previous cognitive schemas such as showing aggression is acceptable, could act as risk factors, especially when they pursue with impulsive style of solving interpersonal problems. As return to beginning of issue as it's known problem-solving skills are vital for preventing aggressive behaviors and violence. With impulsive style of problem solving, individuals accept the first idea and solution that comes to mind, they decide quickly and carelessly and as consequence the solution is inadequate or include violence (Calvete, 2008).

The bullying action which is too common form of violence whether traditional or cyber is dependent on individual personality and contextual factors; but the bullying actions are increased by legal inequalities because they lead to bias and violence (Chetty and Alathur, 2018). Unlike offline predatory crimes which require direct interaction between victims and offenders, cybercrimes do not need direct touches or contact. So, it should be noted that virtual crimes become much more dangerous for people who witness on internet or social media (Hawdon et al., 2015). According to the lawyers One such large and significant new form has created a large number of smaller ones and conditioned the transformation of things and phenomena from the physical world into completely new digital forms. The same happened with violence, as a phenomenon, a pattern of behavior and a part of human nature from the very beginnings of civilization, which took its new form being called a digital violence (Bjelajac and Filipovic, 2021).

4.2. Media and Violence

At this chapter the relationship between media and violence will be explained in the framework of "General Aggression Model" which try to explain term to aggression in terms of developmental, social-cognitive and social learning theories. Also, the traits of personality are important (Allen and Anderson, 2015). With general definition, personality defines as the stereotyped behaviors and knowledge that individuals use to interpret the world and direct their behaviors (Anderson and Bushman, 2002). According to General Aggression Model input is being received, and the aggressive responses given according to the nature of this information are either very intense (aggressive behaviors, provocations) or less intense aggression (such as a high degree of empathy, sitting in the Church) (Parrott, 2008).

Allen and Anderson (2015: 1) consider more biological, social, cognitive, and developmental features of the General Aggression Model than field-specific theories about aggression in the literature. This model considers situational, individual and biological-physiological variables when examining the relationship between the individual and aggression. In this way, concepts such as violence, proactive and reactive aggression, direct and indirect aggression, displaced, repressed, reflected aggression, which have an important place in the studies related to aggression, are explained. Since social behaviors can be learned, they can vary from person to person. However, the General Aggression Model discusses the individual's level of aggression in the context of how he interprets events in a large time, how he reacts characteristically to events, his ability to react differently to events, and his expectations about the consequences of events. These variables are important for the General Aggression Model because it measures how the individual reacts in environments that are alien to him and to which he is accustomed (Wiedemanvd, 2015).

Allen and Anderson (2015) stated that the General Aggression Model can be adapted to any field, but given the transformative power of media, the General Aggression Model is very important for media research. Since the media is questioned at the beginning of the factors that teach violence to society, researchers have studied the effect of violence presented in the media on individuals and societies. But the media has positive effects just like its negative effects. So, the General Aggression Model illuminates the power of the media to present it as "good" or "bad." Ferguson and Dyck (2012) stated that it is not a new idea that individuals who are exposed to aggressive behavior or who are exposed to violence presented in fictional media imitate such behavior, especially that media violence has been presented in books, films, poems and video games since different periods. According to the General Aggression Model, whether it is violence presented in the media in real life or fiction, the individual's frequent exposure to these stimuli can cause him to react aggressively to similar events over time. So, the individual can learn how to react aggressively. Another point is that long-term exposure to violent media products or experiencing violence in real life can also cause the individual to become numb about it. The General Aggression Model suggests that at this point, the individual can form an aggressive personality structure through these violent stimuli to which they are exposed (Ferguson and Dyck, 2012).

In the light of the theory described above, how the concept of media and violence is evaluated by researchers gains importance at this point. With the increase in the popularity of films in America in the 1920s and television in the 1950s, discussions of "media and violence" began. In this process, while some of the society finds the depictions in the media entertaining, some of them think that it triggers the phenomenon of violence in individuals. In the current age of technology, video games have been included in the media elements that trigger violence (Sparks, Sparks and Sparks, 2009).

While it is seen that the studies on the relationship between the media and violence are initially shaped by the question "Does watching violence in the media cause aggressive behaviors?" (Sparks et al, 2009) , it is seen that the debates in the 21st century are now tried to be examined interactively under the light of factors such as cognitive, emotional, behavioral characteristics, genetic predispositions and the triggering environment around them (Funk et al., 2016; Laer, 2014; Li et al., 2016). When considered with the approaches in different disciplines, Bandura's "Social Learning Model (1963)" comes to the fore from a pedagogical point of view. According to this model, the observed negative behaviors are imitated by children, and when the social environment reinforces these behaviors, the behavior increases and when it punishes, the behavior is extinguished (cited in Demirbaş and Yağbasan, 2005).

Before the year 2000, it was seen that the studies on media and violence in the literature focused mainly on television (Lawrence, 1997; Meller, 1996; Pennell and Browne, 1999; Smith and Donnerstein, 1998). It has been determined that current studies are shaped around issues such as video games and violence, and the physiological effects of violence on the brain in the media (Guo, 2013; Hummer, 2014; Kalnin, 2011; Wiedeman, 2015).

According to some researchers, discussions about media and violence are shaped around a one-dimensional, direct relationship between media and violent behaviors in the literature (Meller, 1996), while according to some researchers, the subject of violence presented in the media is a phenomenon with a social, economic and political dimension that has been examined in research for a long time but a general consensus cannot be reached on its causes, effects and dynamics (Huesmann, 2007; Özer and Özer, 2010).

Kalnin et al. (2011) examined brain images (fMRI) of 22 people with aggressive behavior patterns and 22 people without aggressive behavior patterns after exposure to violent media products and found that as a result, individuals had changes in brain imagery, and stated that violent media affected individuals' thinking and emotional response skills.

According to Bushman and Anderson (2002), violence in the media increases the aggressive behavior of individuals, but according to them, the question to be asked today is not whether violence in the media increases aggression in individuals, but "why" violent media increases aggression in individuals.

Many writers and media producers note that if viewers don't find it interesting, less violence will appear in the media (Strasburger et al., 2009). Burton (2005) discussed the media and violence in different dimensions. According to Burton (2005), it is possible to argue that "too much" violence is presented in the media and that this violence has an impact on the social behavior of individuals in society. But since "violent acts" are complex behaviors, it is not possible to blame the media alone. Therefore, Burton (2005) argues that it is easier to blame the media than to blame individuals for their behavior; that it is difficult to accept that the social environment in which the individual grows up and their individual characteristics are more connected with violent behaviors; He stated that it is easier to look for a single cause for problems such as violence, so society is more inclined to blame the media for violent incidents. According to Burton (2005), when discussing the influence of the media on individuals and the issues of violence in the media, one should not start with the social assumption that the media "imposes something" on individuals. At this point, different definitions of violence, the different natures of media products (such as visual images versus written words) and different social-cultural elements related to how the violent content shown is understood should be evaluated. Of course, Burton (2005) states that the presentation of violence is unrelated to the behavior of individuals and that there is no judgment, and similarly, he thinks that the only cause of violence should not be reduced to the media.

Bartholow et al. (2006) stated that many studies have found that exposure to long-term media violence increases aggression in individuals, but that this mechanism that affects the individual is still not defined. According to Strasburger et al. (2009), media exposure to repetitive violent products has an impact on individuals' levels of emotional arousal. Researchers have focused on this issue because the desensitization of individuals to violence, which is seen as entertainment, can result in desensitization to violence in real life (Strasburger et al., 2009). Bartholow (2006) reported that long-term media violence numbs individuals and therefore gives flat, emotionless reactions instead of the necessary reactions to real-life violence. Bartholow (2006), who studies the concept of numbness in the context of the effect of violent video games on the brain, has found that the P300 value (a type of component secreted against certain stimuli in the brain) is less in the brains of individuals who are exposed to violent video games for a long time, that is, individuals are numb to violent events. Carnagey et al. found similar findings to the results of this study in 2007, where they found that individuals who played violent video games for a long time became numb to violent events. Funk et al. (2004) found a significant relationship between violence-only, interactive video games and low empathy skills in their research to measure the relationship between video games, television, internet exposure to 154 students attending the 8th grade and levels of empathy and aggression. Read et al. (2016) found no significant relationship between individuals exposed to violent video games and apathy to violence, contrary to many studies in the literature.

As a result of the study in which Ulaş et al. (2012) examined 200 scientific research on violence in the media in domestic and foreign literature, it was stated that violence in the media was presented in its hidden or open, psychological or physical dimensions, that violence was marketed through the media, that children were most affected by the violence presented in the media and that desensitization to violence occurred. As a result of his study in which he examined the phenomenon of violence in the media in the context of child murder news, Yeğen (2015) stated that the print media should be objective when reporting on violence, that the crime should not be forgotten to be individual, should not make disinformation and should not give unnecessary details. Similarly, İnci (2013) and Pişkin (2008), in their study examining the murders committed under the pretext of honor in the print media, stated that journalists presented violence against women using a male-dominated language and that such news presentations contributed to the continuity of the dominant cultural structure. As stated in their critical media theories, Toker and Altun (2015) have determined that social violence is reproduced through the media with the way news is handled, the language and the visuals they use. In other research on femicides, violence and the presentation of facts in the news in Turkey (Cloud, 2008; Gül and Altındal, 2015; Nephew, 2014). Similar results attract attention, and, in this context, it becomes possible to say that the violence presented in the media has an impact on individuals and society.

Media violence is often discussed within the framework of physically damaging behaviors depicted in a fictional structure, film or television. But the issue of violence in the media is more complicated than this. Of course, there is a difference between cutting a person with a knife and punching him in the jaw. Moreover, the emotional reactions, cultural judgments and meanings of individuals against this violence are also different. Moreover, violence is not only physical, but psychological violence against individuals also affects the audience (Burton, 2005).

According to Hamilton (2000; cited in Özer and Özer, 2010), the definition used in the National Television Violence Survey funded by the National Cable Television Association and conducted in 1998 is the most generally accepted definition of media and violence. Accordingly, media violence refers to the depiction or use of physical force in a very convincing way with the intention of physically harming a living being or group of living things; is the demonstration of physical detrimental consequences against a living being or group of living beings in certain ways and varieties with invisible means of violence. According to this definition, there are three basic descriptions of violence: convincing threat, action, and harmful consequences.

Cantor (2012) states that television, film, and other media programs contain images that may cause anxiety, fear, or even traumatize children and adolescents. Moreover, these harmful effects of the media are more diverse and deeper for end-stage children and adolescents. The diversification of the media, television channels and programs and the ability of people to access these media products at any time of the day thanks to the developing technology are also effective in this. Gvirsman et al. (2016) stated that ideological violence in the media also had an impact on children and adolescents. The concept of "ideological violence in the media" is grouped under the subheadings of supporting war, perceiving someone else's race/ethnicity as a threat, and displaying aggressive attitudes toward the normative thoughts of that person or group. Gvirsman et al. (2016) worked with 1,207 Israeli and Palestinian participants to determine the long-term effects of ideological violence in the media and found that children and adolescents who experienced prolonged political violence were more supportive of war.

Bushman and Huesmann (2012) stated that the studies carried out can only measure the effect of the media on aggressive behavior and violence in a one-dimensional way, and that the relationship between violence and crime reflected in the media cannot be reduced to a single factor, and that this issue should be examined at the social and individual level. In addition, thanks to the developments in the media, individuals can use the media as multitasking (multiple operations; using more than one type of media at the same time) and they can reach the images and textual elements containing violence and aggression much more easily.

Violence research related to the media started to be carried out under the concept of television and violence in 1946, and then in 1972, the relationship between television and violence was accepted. In studies from 1972 to 2002, 342 research were conducted to examine the relationship between television and violence and a total of 51 thousand 597 participants were included in this research (Rigel, 2008). Although the issue of violence in the media is mainly associated with television, research shows that on average, a child witnesses 13,000 violent acts on television until the age of 16. Monitoring violent acts can increase mental tension in children and adolescents and weaken impulsive and emotional control in children who are more easily balanced and prone to anger (Yavuzer, 2004). Florea (2013) states that the study of television and violence takes place in two main dimensions: violence in informational publications such as news and fictional violence in publications such as movies and TV series.

Children and adults can learn and imitate violent behaviors by observing people as role models in their social environments (Nar, 2014). In the 21st century, according to the researchers, one of the factors that greatly affected violence and aggression (Nar, 2014; Teyfur, 2014) comes to the media, violence is presented as a very usual concept in the media. Çamlıca (2010) emphasized that children watch horror films and enjoy horror films and stated that the point to be considered is "learning by seeing," that people learn what they see and apply what they learn.

According to Erdal (2012), although the phenomenon of violence in the media is one of the most studied topics in the literature, there is no consensus on the issue. Over time, different models have emerged in the media to perceive violence and to interpret the effects of violence on individuals. In these models, new media technologies are mainly associated with general concerns about individuals considered to be in the risk group, beliefs that violence in the media causes other social problems, the use of consumer concerns by people known to the public, and strategies used to evade regulation (Trend, 2008).

Florea (2013) examined the catharsis effect of violence in the media, especially violence presented on television; First, the logic of the glorious entertainment world of television and its own nature will be deciphered, and then when the mental and cultural structure of society is understood, it will be exposed. But this research is valid for classical media. For new media the issue of violence is much deeper and more pervasive. Due to the structure of new media it's a place where violence could be committed much more easily than the real world. Now, we will examine the issue of new media and violence.

4.2.1. New Media and Violence

Just like media literacy, traditional media has evolved with the development of technology and led to the emergence of the concept of new media. In new communication environments called new media, especially the storage and dissemination of information has become much easier, while at the same time the concept of cyber-violence has led to the emergence of the concept. In addition, the presence of intense and continuous violent stimuli in the traditional media leads individuals to emotional deafness, desensitization and alexithymia, and it is seen that new media can trigger this situation. This part of the research aims to discuss the phenomenon of violence in new media in the context of cyber-violence, its alexithymia and its impact on the justification of cyber-violence, which is the main subject of this study.

5. CYBER-VIOLENCE

Cyber-violence refers to any behavior on the internet advocating violence or using language calculated to inflame the passions to achieve mass emotional catharsis, which can be considered an extension of social violence to the internet. Moreover, due to rapid development of social media and growth of social media users and individuals begin to use social media as a second living place, cyber-violence incidents on social media have appeared frequently, including such behavior as bullying, flaming, and verbal abuse and even deaths (Fan, Huang, Qalati, Shah, Ostic and Pu, 2021: 1). Cyber-violence not always an "event" that occur between two individuals. For today mostly it happens toward "others" such as immigrants. It is another issue that should be discussed under term of diversity and immigrants.

Today, for the 21st century diversity is discussed among many of the countries and cultures. In the "digitalized world" borders between cultures are invisible and dysfunctional due to the structure of digital environment. Especially in social media and other digital environments which offer an opportunity for interaction among users (such as online game platforms or navigations), individuals have chance to get information about other cultures. In terms of social cohesion at both offline and online worlds, those encounters with other cultures are vital, because they can trigger racism, hate speech or other risks about immigrants and refugees. However, those encounters are not always "negative" or "risky." For some individuals to get information about immigrants or refugees could have a chance to break negative perceptions about those people or cultural diversity. Moreover, researchers and policy makers concerned about the challenges of cultural diversity and social cohesion in offline world and online world. They urged to society to support digital citizenship skills of youths at global levels and empower cohesive societies which is so important for cultural diversity (Harris and Johns, 2020).

Cultural diversity is vital issue for technological age, and it is directly related with social cohesion. Social cohesion and digital life are psychosocial phenomenon and mostly related with both offline and online world. However, it also includes hate speeches toward immigrants, trolls who produce fake news and hate speeches and how individuals justify those speeches in both offline and online world. We cannot discuss cultural diversity and social cohesion without immigrants and hate speeches toward those people. Cultural diversity should seem like a variety and harmony for the society though shared identity.

But unfortunately, as a result of hate speeches and dehumanization toward immigrants, cultural diversity mostly seems challenging for society. For example, for American society it is more divided than ever before and there is subtle gap between different policies of left and right wings. Moreover, there is growing hostility between different groups as well (Haroon, Chhabra, Liu, Mohapatra, Shafiq and Wojcieszak, 2022).

According to the findings, countries have difficulty while integrating immigrants to society. Both immigrants and public have prejudice toward each other, due to social media effect. On social media trolls and some racist people have chances to express their "pathological" beliefs and ideas. Sometimes they write fake news about immigrants sometimes about host countries. All individuals are exposed to cyber-harassment and after a while it becomes a violence loop: First both immigrants and host country public are exposed to cyber-harassment, then they normalize those cyber-harassments and finally they justify those cyber-harassments toward immigrants or public. As a result of this social cohesion would be failed.

There are also some other factors that affect justification of cyber-violence which are moral judgments and moral values. Moral judgments and moral values are vital for prosocial behaviors which are the core factors about trigger the commit or justify cyber-violence.

Moral development which starts at early ages and shaped by society and family, have strong relationship with prosocial behaviors in terms of predicting (Zeng, Zhao, Long et al., 2020). This means that strong and well-established moral values are not only beneficial for individuals but also for society.

Before explaining the relationship between moral values and prosocial behaviors, defining prosocial behaviors would be better. According to Zeng et all (2020: 1) prosocial behaviors are voluntary behaviors that are aimed to benefit others or to promote interpersonal harmony. Examples about prosocial behaviors are sharing resources, helping and comforting others. For violence, hate crimes or discrimination toward immigrants, prosocial behaviors have vital and key roles.

Moral judgment consists of evaluations of good and bad, positive and negative. Evaluations represent one of the most basic human responses, can be easily transferred from one object to another through evaluative conditioning and can be made about virtually anything: from written characters, sounds, and objects all the way to human decisions, unintended outcomes, persons, and groups (Malle, 2021: 294). Those moral judgments not only effect the individuals lives but also whole society in terms of immigrants especially. Immigrants' social cohesion is very important to society's behaviors and attitudes toward them. Moreover, on social media there are so many fake news and disinformation toward immigrants and users could be easily manipulated at social media. Individuals' daily lives and digital lives could affect each other. So, if individuals feel that immigrants are not socially integrated, they more tend to be manipulated by social media and justify the violence toward immigrants.

Now, it is time to explain social cohesion.

Social cohesion or social inclusion encapsulate homogeneity, shared values, common purpose in society and sense of belonging (Harris and Johns, 2020). All those values are important, but sense of belonging is vital. Without sense of belonging immigrants mostly feel themselves as "secondary citizen" and they are not supposed to do something for society. For unity in the society active citizenship, full participation and sense of belonging are indispensable. If immigrants are presented as "demons" how these people feel as part of society? Moreover, those presentations as demons can lead to dehumanization of immigrants which makes those people as "hate" target. On social media, immigrants also described with violent extremism, violent nationalism and terrorism. This is also another core concept that effects justification of cyber-violence.

The most important issue about social cohesion is undoubtably violent extremism and terrorism. Due to as immigrants presented as subject of violent extremism and terrorism on social media and televisions, most of the people especially in west countries develop islamophobia. Moreover, racism, discrimination and bias are key factors for risks of social cohesion and can be source for loosing sense of belonging (Harris and Johns, 2020).

Extremism is both political and religious ideology and mostly it is same as terrorism. According to Liebman (cited in Chetty and Alathur, 2018: 109) extremism is "a desire to expand the scope, detail and strictness of religious law, social isolation and the rejection of the surrounding culture." According to Hawdon, Oksanen and Rasanen (2015) online extremist and hate materials are type of cyber-violence. Due to this classification, they argued that cyber-violence includes online materials that express extreme views of hatred toward specific group or individual. This kind of cyber-violence not only includes hatred but also separation, defamation, deception and hostility toward "others" by using information and communication technologies (ICTs). As consequences, anybody who can use ICT make target anyone about cyber-violence because of their ethnicity, religion, race, gender, sexual orientation or some other group-defining characteristic is disseminating online hate or extremist ideas (Hawdon et al., 2015).

For extremist materials there is big confusion. People who post and prepare extremist materials see those materials as educational not criminal. This discrimination is very important due to justify extremist activities. They intend with the word "educational" as they give information to others about their group or ideology (Hawdon et al., 2015).

While talking about extremism we should talk about radicalization because radicalization covers the terms "justification." As a definition radicalization means "change in beliefs, feelings, and behaviors in directions that increasingly justify intergroup violence and demand sacrifice in defense of the group" (McCauley and Moskalenko, 2008: 416). Radicalization is mostly discussed with the term "identity." Wang, Platow, Bar-Tal, Augoustinos, Rooy and Spears (2022: 457) explained this identity concept with the framework of Social Identity Approach. The Social Identity Approach comprises both social identity theory (Tajfel and Turner, 1986) and self-categorization theory (Turner et al., 1987). Basically, The Social Identity Approach underlines social-psychological concepts to understand group-based processes. The core concept of the theory is to recognize that people not only have identities as unique individuals (their personal identities), but as group members as well (their social identities). That is people's social identities—their psychological representation of themselves with others rather than separate from others—that have been linked to a range of social behaviors, such as the expression of in-group favoritism, helping, trust and social influence (Wang et al., 2021: 457–458). Immigrants mostly seen as "group-based identity," they are not described with their personal characteristics or identity.

With raising of internet, extremists find a new place to spread their ideas and beliefs. According to Gerstenfeld, Phyllis, Diana, Grant and Chau-Pu (2003) extremists have four objectives at online environments: Increase their international attractiveness, recruit new members, network and close relationships with like-minded groups, deal with image and public opinion. Internet and other digital environments are seen as instrumental for extremists to conduct and pursue psychological warfare; produce, publish and spread propaganda; to spread dangerous and sensitive data like mine effect on society; raise and finds funds and collect resources; not only recruit but also mobilize new supporters and followers (Weimann, 2006; Winter, Neumann, Meleagrou-Hitchens, Ranstorp, Vidino and Fürst, 2020). Digital environments make easy to show cyber-violence toward immigrants. Now, we should turn the subject of cyber-harassment toward immigrants. Cyber-harassment is an umbrella term that covers polarization, radicalization and hate speech also.

Although there are different factors that affect polarization, radicalization and hate crime but the rise of social media seems the trigger factors. With "loop effect" which means to users on social media tend to follow the other users in their social network, the users stuck in this loop, and it also make major contribution to polarization. Moreover, online exposure and behaviors not only explained by social homophily and individual bias but also by algorithms. So, it could be said that at online environments it could be easy to create radicalization, foster civil unrest and endanger public health (Haroon et al., 2022).

The European Court of Human Rights (cited in Chetty and Alathur, 2018: 110) defined hate speech under the umbrella of all forms of expression which spread, incite, promote or justify racial hatred, xenophobia, anti-semitism. It is clear that speech toward immigrants make easier to physical violence toward those people.

Social cohesion should be long-standing. For this reason, researchers defined some risky situations for social inclusion such as limited intercultural contact, racism and lack of urged of pluralism (Harris and Johns, 2020). Among of those risky factors racism which can be exaggerate through hate speeches and dehumanization via social media is key dimension for cyber-harassment for both online and offline worlds.

Individuals' social media practices could not be evaluated without civic and political processes in both offline and online worlds.

When we are talking about immigrants generally first thing that come to mind are Muslims and unfortunately, they are demonized and vilified online with negative attitudes, and stereotypes with an intention of creating violence. Increasing online abuse toward Muslim immigrants also need to address Islamophobia. Generally, people think that hijab is a sign for individuals' integration level which are not related to each other. But unfortunately, this misinterpretation and confusion could lead to avoid gaining awareness to public about Islamic culture. At digital platforms hostility and aggression against Muslims is done by the actions such as cyberbullying, harassment, incitement or threats that could turn easily to offline violence or encourage perpetrators for any offline violence or physical attack (Chetty and Alathur, 2018).

At 2022 February, Russian invasion of Ukraine seems to reveal the hypocrisy of media in terms of racism and immigrants. According to Polonska-Kimunguyi (2022) the western media's attitude toward Ukraine immigrants and other immigrants from Somalis, Ethiopia, Syria, Palestine etc. are different. It is too bad that, she argued that the media seen refuges from Middle East or Aisa less newsworthy, their predicament as undeserving of other peoples' attention. Moreover, in UK according to "migration crisis" report, public see refuges as the source of crime and violence. Unfortunately, it is same for the rest of the world. In this situation media has an important role as re-created old speeches and divide humans into "us" and "them" which is so dangerous for healthy and peaceful society. Polonska-Kimunguyi (2022) also talked about the hypocrisy of Western about Ukrainians Refugees. According to her, Ukrainians are not seen as migrants by the Western Media. Actually, they are seen as people not a thread for the society. They are caring for their homeland, and they have useful skills for the society. Western media evaluate Ukrainians like that. That is really shame for the media.

According to the research (Hawdon, Oksanen and Rasanen, 2015) there is a gap between real and virtual world experiences. Maybe we could see this gap obviously in online extremism. Moreover, it is well documented in literature that those who are victimized once are more likely to be victimized again in both virtual and real worlds. The most dangerous risk about online extremism is hate speech. Unfortunately, some innocent immigrants could be blamed to being extremist. We have to deeply analyzed hate speech toward immigrants because those extremists and hate speech could lead to justification cyber-violence.

Hate speech, which is defined as "offensive kind of communication mechanism that expresses an ideology of hate using stereotypes" (Chetty and Alathur, 2018: 108). Through hate speeches, perpetrators generally target different characteristics such as gender, religion, race, and special needs. Today, hate speech is seemed as common and powerful global threats (Chetty and Alathur, 2018).

On social media especially on Twitter, direct hate speech words toward immigrants are so rare. Generally, the foul language, false or doubtful information about immigrants, irony, distasteful speech, humiliation or contempt, psychological or physical threats, provocation to violence (Calderon, Vega and Herrero, 2020). Those hate speeches which are bias-motivated, hostile and malicious are much more harmful for victims due to hate speech is more destructive and have more impact related to race, ethnicity, religion, sexual orientation, occupation, gender or special needs have more impact than the individuals' personal information (Chetty and Alathur, 2018).

There is another point about hate speech that, sometimes hate speech is considered as a shortcut way to get instant popularity at online environments without showing more effort (Chetty and Alathur, 2018).

The impact of hate speech is not same on all occasions; its impact is depended on person involved, content of hate speech, location of the occasion, and circumstances (Chetty and Alathur, 2018).

Hate speech could harm the victims directly or indirectly. At direct hate speech the victims are injured or effected immediately. But indirect hate speech like racism in digital environments might trigger and motivated other racists to commit violence, harassment and intimidation toward victim through identity (Chetty and Alathur, 2018).

The further part of hate speech is "hate crime" unfortunately. While hate speech is done by posting a message on social media or other digital environments, hate crime is defined as hate-motivated physical attack. The key relation between them is social network: Through social media networks hate crime perpetrators can plan and execute the attacks (Chetty and Alathur, 2018).

Hate speech, immediately after the event will flow heavily on social networks, after few days will get reduced, after some more days reduces to zero level and after a long time once again it may appear (Chetty and Alathur, 2018).

Unfortunately, immigrants suffer from hate speech in terms of racism. Although racism has a subtle definition, according to Eva Polonska-Kimunguyi (2022) media has a specific role to creation of race and racial divisions. So, we could say that youths mostly use social media are under risk about this manipulation in terms of racism.

Different from cyberbullying, online extremist and hate material goals to abuse at a collective identity rather than a specific individual (Howdon et al., 2015).

6. JUSTIFICATION OF CYBER-HARASSMENT

For a long time, ICTs have served as important tools for both interaction and entertainment (Linares, Aranda, Garcia-Domingo, Amezcua, Fuentes and Moreno-Padilla, 2021). But of course, like any other technologies, ICTs are not so innocent tools. They could be used manipulation of individuals, spreading hate speech or cyber-bully to others. All of those actions are "seen" actions. That means, people could easily aware that which are hate speech or cyber-harassment and which are not. But justifying harassment is something different.

Justification of violence is an important issue that has been worked in the frame of physical and traditional violence. According to the researchers (Borrajo, Gamez-Guadix and Calvete, 2015; Anderson et al, 2003) among men who justify violence, those beliefs about violence were important predictor of physical violence. Moreover, they claimed that women generally justify psychological violence toward their partner whereas men justify physical violence toward their partner. Commonly, justification of violence, beliefs and attitudes toward violence are studied about romantic relationships, dating or in marriages. But there is not enough study about justification of violence, extremism or online harassment especially toward immigrants.

Justification of violence is not only explained by different factors but also it is explained with antisocial behaviors which are defined as overt aggressive behaviors such as fighting, arguing, and any other deviant behaviors (Loeber and Schmaling, 1985; cited in Calvete, 2008: 1083). The most specific characteristic of antisocial behaviors is they can predict various problems related with violence and aggression in adult life. Moreover, not only antisocial behaviors but also proactive aggression and behavior problems are associated with childhood narcissism in which individuals evaluate themselves as superior and inflated sense of entitlement (Calvete, 2008).

Beside of antisocial behaviors there are some theories that helped to explain justification of cyber-harassment. Of course, only theories or behavioral explanations are not enough to clarify the justification of cyber-harassment especially toward immigrants. They are not enough but needed. By the way, those theories also explained aggressive behaviors which are vital to understand and explain justification of violence.

First theory is Social Information Processing Theory. This theory is related with how mental operations affect behavioral responding in social situations

(Dodge and Rabiner, 2004). Social-cognitive approaches are important to understand maladaptive behaviors (Danila, Balazsi and Baban, 2022).

According to the social information processing (SIP) model, the social-cognitive processes can be organized in six subsequent steps. The first two steps refer to the selection and interpretation of social cues: encoding (which cues are registered) and interpretation (interpreting the combined meaning of all registered cues). For example, perceiving someone's facial expression without any interpretation is part of the encoding step, whereas thinking about why someone is laughing contains a subjective component and is therefore an interpretation. A feedback loop exists between encoding and interpretation; such that interpretation can influence encoding of subsequent social cues. The last four SIP-steps refer to cognitive processes which enable an individual to form a behavioral response: goal selection, construction of possible responses, response choice, and the execution of the chosen response. Finally, each person has a database which includes memories, schemas, and social knowledge that influence each SIP-step. For example, if people get to know each other (knowledge and memories), the interpretation of the other's intentions will improve. While the database concurrently influences the SIP-steps, it is also simultaneously updated with new experiences. The updated database, in turn, influences future encoding, interpretation, and behavioral responses, possibly leading to the development of negative spirals. Victims are likely to have difficulties in sending and interpreting social information, as they seem to have poorer social cognition and social skills (Kellij, Lodder, Bedem, Güroğlu and Veenstra, 2022: 288). The key point is that, when aggressive behaviors and their usage become acceptable, it predicts anti-social behavior which is very dangerous for society. Schemas which are related with cognitive structures and if they tend to justify violence, showing violent behavior is much easier (Calvete, 2008). Moreover, within the framework of socio-technical perspective, at social media there are bystander effects, and it helps to reshaped individuals like society interaction (Wong, Cheung, Xiao and Thatcher, 2021). So, according to SIP Model individuals' schemas which can be shaped by society is important for justification of cyber-violence. Moreover, there is another model that related with justification of violence: Belief in a Just World Theory.

The Theory on the Belief in a Just World indicates that individuals have a need to believe that they live in a just world. This belief is divided into the personal belief in a just world (PBJW) and the general belief in a just world (GBJW). The PBJW refers to the belief that the world is fair to oneself; the GBJW refers to the belief that the world is fair to other people. For example, people feel that "I get what I deserve" when they have high PBJW, while they feel that "people get what they deserve" when they have high GBJW (Wang, Wang, Liu, Yang, Zheng and Bai, 2021: 2).

In terms of justification of violence especially from point of victims' view, a just world is one in which good things happen to good people and bad things happen to bad people. Threats to JWB, such as an innocent victim experiencing a violent attack, are intolerable and necessitate alterations in the individual's perception of the victim so that the victim becomes deserving of the tragedy (Pincotti and Orcutt, 2021: 260).

Before explaining the negative effects of justification cyber-harassment, we should explain how exposure of cyber-violence effect behaviors of individuals. According to research that conducted at Finland (cited in Hawdon et al., 2015: 30) Finnish Facebook users who visited websites that promote suicide or self-mutilation were more likely to be exposed to online hate materials than those who did not visit such sites. The important point is according to term of desensitization, individuals who more exposed to dangerous materials become normalize that violence and after a while they start to show those type of behaviors. In another study with Facebook users showed that (cited in Hawdon et al., 2015: 31) young Facebook users who produced hate materials were over four times more likely to be exposed to hate materials as compared to those who did not produce hate materials.

While the concept of justification is generally evaluated as a legal phenomenon, this concept is evaluated in the context of the effect of communication tools on social and political legitimacy within the framework of communication and media. For the social legitimacy order, the phenomenon of socialization, which is defined as adopting the values, symbols and rules of the society to which they belong, to individuals comes first. Studies on mass media in the literature also emphasize the impact of mass media on socialization (Anık, 2014).

Although the phenomenon of violence, which is defined as a violation of human rights, has existed throughout history, some forms of violence have been legitimized by different communities in different time periods and in different ways. Especially with the increase in studies and awareness about human rights and their general acceptance, the types of violence that gained legitimacy began to be questioned (Baran et al., 2012). Violence can also be seen as a phenomenon that is either instinctive or influenced only by environmental factors (Moses, 1996). While some researchers explain violence in terms of the attachment relationship that the individual establishes with their parents in childhood (Bowlby, 2012), some researchers state that the human being is born with "disease" at birth.

Studies on the recognition of violence as a legitimate right are in different dimensions. While Giddens (2008) discusses violence within the totalitarian state system, in 1953 Westley appears to have discussed violence within the framework of the police's use of violence as a legitimate right. In this context, Westley (1953) stated that they considered it acceptable and moral for police to use violence.

Arendt (2016) states that the 20th century is a century of wars and revolutions, that is, violence, and that the destructive potential of the means of violence with technological development is superior to political ends. Unlike power, force, and the use of force, violence requires means to realize itself. According to Arendt (2016), the actual use of violent means in armed conflicts cannot be justified. At this point, Arendt (2016) states that human behavior is unpredictable, and that violence contains an element of "arbitrariness."

Moses (1996) sees the legitimization of violence by a society or group as a crucial problem. Especially when the concept of nation is considered, according to Moses (1996), in some cases nations ask the individual to act on behalf of the nation and even order it. Even if this request or order involves a violent act, violence can be justified when it is in the name of the nation. Akkanat (2011) states that types of violence such as state violence, war, terrorism, xenophobia and racism are tried to be explained in a psychological, physiological or anthropological framework, which is reduced to the level of a phenomenon accepted as "norm" violence. Çoklar & Meşe (2014) discussed the legitimization of violence through rape myths and stated that sexist attitudes and the legitimization of the gender-related system played an important role in the emergence and acceptance of rape myths that are widely accepted at the social level.

Pabian and Vandebosch (2016) investigated the relationship between adolescents' witnessing cyberbullying and their moral values, empathy and tolerance for cyberbullying. They worked with 1,412 students between the ages of 10–13 in two steps at 6 months' intervals and as a result of the research, it was found that the empathy skills of the students who witnessed cyberbullying in step 1 were adversely affected in the 6-month period, but their attitudes about cyberbullying were not related to witnessing cyberbullying in step 1.

Koçer (2015) conducted a two-stage study to examine the effect of some factors in violent video games on aggressive behavior after playing games. The first study compared the effect of violent and non-violent games and found no significant differences on aggressive behavior. In the second part of the study, the legitimacy of violence and the effect of finding a stereotypical target on post-game aggression were investigated. In the second part of the study, it was determined that the level of post-game aggression increased when a stereotypical target was found with violence that was considered legitimate and when a stereotypical target was found with violence that was not seen as legitimate. In this sense, it is possible to say that the study is not compatible with other studies in the literature.

Laer (2014) designed a two-stage experiment to examine the effects of cyber-violence on users on social media under situations where users feel adequate and acceptable. In his experiment, Laer (2014) emphasized the dilemma that the social media user can easily reveal his social identity and the other user can use his right to be protected from cyber-violence. In this direction, 124 students conducted an experiment with 357 participants, including 233 students in the 1st experiment and 233 students in the 2nd experiment, and the participants were taught stories about cyber-violence in computer environment in the form of presentations. In the first experiment, only stories about cyber-violence were taught, while at the beginning of the 2nd experiment, participants were asked whether they had experienced cyber-violence before. As a result of the research, a positive correlation was found between the participants' perceptions of having information about cyber-violence that affected them personally in the presentation format and their perceptions of taking fair measures against cyber-violence for both experiments.

Krcmar and Valkenburg (1999) developed a scale called the Moral Interpretation of Interpersonal Violence Scale (MIIV) and conducted a study using 12 different stories with 158 children to measure how children justified violence. They asked the children to explain the "violence" they perceived in the stories for how right and wrong they found it. It has been found that children who watch a lot of fictional/fantasy violence interpret the violence in the stories as less wrong, but children who watch more realistic violence interpret the violence in the stories as more wrong. In addition, children who watched more fictional violence used less moral justification when explaining the reason for their judgment in children who followed realistic violence.

The connection between the justification of violence and alexithymia is explained by Funk et al. (2004) based on the individual's way of thinking. The emotionally deaf individual may not be able to evaluate the moral or moral aspect of the issue when he decides or takes action. Because, in particular, the concept of violence has been internalized a lot by the individual and has now been accepted as normal. Therefore, it is not possible for him to make a healthy assessment of his decisions or actions (Funk et al., 2004). The point that is particularly emphasized here is that the individual's exposure to violence not only in real life but also through the media gives the same effect (Funk et al., 2004).

7. EMOTIONAL DEAFNESS (ALEXITIMIA) AND VIOLENCE AT MEDIA

When both foreign and domestic sources are examined, the concept of Emotional Deafness (Alexitimitis) has been seen as a concept that is mainly evaluated within the field of psychiatry (Bekker et al., 2007; Craparo et al., 2014; Zimmermann, 2006). Alexithymia (Emotional Deafness), which has been found in many studies as an explanatory for susceptibility to violence, aggressive behavior, and antisocial behaviors (Velotti et al., 2016; Bekker et al., 2007) was first described by Sifneos in 1967 and translated into our language as "Absence of Words for Emotions." The most basic feature of alexithymia is a decrease in awareness of emotions, difficulty in expressing emotions, inability to establish a relationship between emotion and thought, inability to name emotions, difficulty in using life and body language that is very mechanical (Aydın et al., 2013). Bekker et al. (2007) stated that the concept of emotional deafness negatively affects the ability to connect with other people, and that being open to relationships is functional, but the inability to connect will also affect the emotional deafness rate of the individual.

Alexithymia, which is tried to be explained under concepts such as numbness and inability to react to individuals who are heavily exposed to media violence in the communication literature, has started to be examined under a separate title in recent studies and has been measured mainly in the context of the relationship between violence in video games and emotional deafness of the individual. Excessive exposure to violence presented in the media "numbs" individuals, according to Strasburger et al. (2009). Here, researchers have used the concept of numbness to mean that emotional responses to a certain stimulus are not given after a certain period of exposure, just as it is applied to phobic patients in clinics. For example, a patient with a phobia toward dogs is exposed to dogs in a clinical environment and under appropriate conditions, and eventually gets used to sick dogs, so that his fear disappears. In this context, exposure to violent elements can cause the same numbness in individuals through the media (Strasburger et al., 2009).

Alexithymia is evaluated in two different ways, regardless of exposure to real-life violence or violence in the media. The first is emotional alexithymia. In this case, the individual is suppressing his emotions or acting insensitively in situations where he should react emotionally under normal circumstances.

In cognitive alexithymia, there are beliefs and thoughts that violence is a very normal and inevitable phenomenon in the individual (Funk et al., 2004).

Emotional deafness (alexithymia) can occur not only through daily or real-life violence, but also through images of violence viewed in the media. Desensitization to violence is not immediately noticeable; it is considered to be the result of repeated exposure to real-life violence or violence in the media. Although in the 21st century studies are carried out on children and adolescents exposed to violence in new technology tools such as video games and the internet, the results of the study conducted by Molitor and Hirsch in 1994 confirm the results: watching violence increases tolerance for violence (akt. Funk et al., 2004).

Another discussion about numbness or desensitization is whether this desensitization will affect the individual's involvement or intervention in a violent incident. In an experiment conducted by Thomas and Drabman (1975: cited in Strasburger, 2009: 176) 1st and 3rd grade students were shown violent and non-violent TV programs and then the behavior of two preschool children was watched. Children who watched violent TV programs when preschoolers fought were significantly slower than children who did not watch violent TV programs and sought solutions or help. In addition, more than half of the children who watched violent TV programs did not leave the room or go to call adults, even though they were told that the fight could end when they called an adult.

Arıcak and Özbay (2016) conducted research on the expression of cyber-bullying, cyber-victimization, emotional deafness and anger. In their research with 1,257 high school students continuing their education in Istanbul, they found that students' emotional deafness and chronic anger rates and internet usage time increased their victimization rates of cyberbullying. As a result of the research conducted by Akın (2014) with 100 high school students and 105 university students to measure the relationship between internet addiction and alexithymia and mood regulation, they found that alexithymia, emotion regulation difficulty and impulsivity are explanatory of internet addiction and at the same time, emotion regulation skills and alexithymia play a mediating role in internet addiction. Zimmermann (2006) examined the relationship between emotional deafness and crime susceptibility of male adolescents in the 14–18 age group. In this study, Zimmermann, who worked with 36 adolescents who were pushed to crime and male adolescents who had not committed 46 crimes, revealed that the emotional deafness rates of adolescents pushed to crime were significantly higher and that they came from broken families. In this context, Zimmermann stated that emotional deafness and family structure factors are strong determinants of susceptibility to crime.

In terms of the relationship between violence and emotional deafness, in societies where violent events occur, violence is accustomed to a certain period of time and individuals become desensitized to news about violent acts (Moses, 1996). The individual's reaction to dangerous situations with the urge to survive; trying to protect himself, taking action, sometimes exhibiting aggressive behaviors, feeling bad is vital for him to continue his life. However, while these reactions are not seen in emotionally deaf individuals, the ability to be aware of their own emotions is also destroyed (Velotti et al., 2016).

In the 21st century, with the increase in brain studies and providing more concrete data to researchers, fMRI and PET Scan studies have started to be used interdisciplinarity. Kelly et al. (2007) of the Department of Radiology at Columbia University repeatedly examined the lateral orbitofrontal cortex in the brains of individuals exposed to media violence. Activation disorder in this region of the brain causes people to lose control over their behavior and exhibit aggressive behaviors. At the end of the experiment, the researchers found that repeated exposure to violent images reduced activation in these areas. However, the main finding of the experiment is that short-term exposure to violent images causes underwork in these areas.

Long-term exposure of children, especially children, to violence in the media or in real life causes them to condition their emotional reactions (Bushman and Huesmann, 2012: 239). With the classical conditioning in learning theories, the individual is exposed to a specific stimulus (fever, chocolate, etc.). He learns to develop emotions such as fear, anger, joy. The emergence of such emotions is a behavior that is learned in daily life regardless of environments such as the media. For example, if you touch the fire, your hand will burn, and it hurts. A person who sees such situations happen to other individuals in the media (advertisements, movies, video games, etc.) may experience the same kind of emotions. Individuals who are repeatedly exposed to media products containing emotionally intense stimuli cannot react to such situations after a while. This is called "desensitization" and is often associated with the inability to respond psychologically to depictions of violence in the media (Bushman and Huesmann, 2012). For example, even children who are exposed to long-term exposure to situations that naturally make the person feel uncomfortable, such as seeing blood and watching violent events, become emotionless. Violent content in the media causes emotional deafness and can increase aggressive behavior in individuals exposed to these violent contents. In other words, when the individual is exposed to disturbing images, he can behave aggressively but does not feel "emotion" (Bushman and Huesmann, 2012; Sparks, Sparcks Sparks, 2002). The concept of emotional deafness is that after the individual is exposed to repeated violence through the media, gets used to this situation, internalizes it and provides psychological satisfaction, it cannot show emotions such as anxiety, anger and anger where it should be shown (Sparks and Sparks, 2002). The biggest negative consequence of apathy to violence in the media is increased tolerance for violence in real life (Sparks, Sparks and Sparks, 2002). As individuals' dull reactions to violence increase, violent behavior will increase in society. Because individuals no longer perceive violent behaviors as behaviors that need to be reacted to and stopped (Sparks and Sparks, 2002).

The main question of the Theory of Desensitization, which is included in the theories of communication, is the extent to which mass media interact with increasing insignificance "too much," reducing experiences and even lowering moral-moral standards (DeFleur, 2010). The mass media offers intense stimulus and acclimates people to many situations; increased crime rates, the reduction or loss of sexual norms, the use of dirty language in general, the shaking of family values and children's rights are criticized (Funk et al., 2004). From the point of view of societies, individuals are against mass media, offensive popular music, thoughtless news, clichéd conspiracy scenarios in movies, the use of abusive language and disgusting websites; they even state that they think that online communication, which replaces real communication today, is meaningless and harmful. However, despite all these criticisms and evaluations—except for exceptional times – the print media, films, journalists, and internet media are slowly but steadily degrading cultural life, behavioral norms and moral values (DeFleur, 2010).

As can be seen, the legitimization of cyber-violence is a layered and interactive phenomenon that cannot be explained by one dimension and one discipline. Therefore, it is necessary to evaluate the legitimization of cyber-violence through both communication, psychology, pedagogy and social effects, and in the studies in the literature given above, the effects of violence on the brain structure of individuals are now studied in the media in a physiological context.

In the second part of this book how the justification of cyberbullying is examined will be presented within the framework of the research design.

PART II

8. A RESEARCH ABOUT JUSTIFICATION OF CYBER-HARASSMENT AMONG TURKISH YOUTHS

8.1. Aim and Scope of the Research

The aim of this study is to investigate the relationship between individuals' digital media literacy skills and justification of cyber-harassment. In this context, digital media literacy, the frequency of social media use and attitudes toward social media will be examined, and the effect of this attitude and frequency of use on individuals applying cyber-violence and being exposed to cyber-violence is revealed. In the emerging framework, how individuals perceive cyber-violence and how this perception explains the emotional deafness levels of individuals were investigated and the effect of all these relationships on justification of cyber-harassment was discussed. The research questions of this research, which examined the relationship between adolescents' digital media literacy skills and their experiences toward cyber-violence and the effect of emotional deafness on the justification of cyber-violence for adolescents, are as follows:

Research question 1: Is there a relationship between digital media literacy and emotional deafness?

Research question 2: Is there a relationship between being cyberbullied and presenting cyberbullying behavior?

Research question 3: Is there a relationship between exposure to cyberbullying and the levels of alexithymia in adolescents?

Research question 4: Is there a relationship between exhibiting cyberbullying behavior and adolescents' levels of alexithymia?

The perception of violence and the perspective of violence is an interdisciplinary issue that is discussed not only for media studies but also in many areas of social sciences. In the current information technology era, intense information bombardment causes individuals to become emotionally "deaf" and specially to normalize news about violence. The normalization of violence may lead individuals to perceive violence as legitimate and to see violence as a legitimate right. It is thought that the first step in front of violence prevention programs or helping individuals exposed to violence is to create awareness on a societal basis that violence cannot be legitimate. Therefore, media literacy and information literacy are skills that should be gained not only to children and young people, but also to media consumers in the whole society.

With this research, the factors affecting individuals' perception of violence as a legitimate right were evaluated within the framework of digital media literacy and emotional deafness. In this context, rather than presenting only relational findings on the media and the perception of violence, the interaction between the perception of violence in the virtual environment as a legitimate right by individuals and the frequency of cyber-violence has been revealed.

8.2. Design of the Research

The research was applied face-to-face to students who continued their university education in Istanbul between June and September 2016. Before the face-to-face form was filled out, the students were announced that they would participate in the research on a voluntary basis and their verbal consent was obtained.

8.3. Sample of Research and Data Collection Tools

The universe of the study consists of 1.2.3.ve 4th grade students who continue their university education in Istanbul. On a voluntary basis, 400 university students (206 female and 194 male) participated in the study. In order to measure the perception of information literacy, emotional deafness and violence to the students who participated in the research on a voluntary basis; The Digital Literacy Assessment Scale, Toronto Alexithymia (Emotional Deafness) Scale, Revised Cyberbullying Inventory and questions prepared by the researcher to legitimize cyber-violence were applied.

Digital Literacy Assessment Scale is a scale developed by Acar (2015) and is a 5-point likert-type scale consisting of 41 items in total. The scale consists of five factors and these factors are; awareness, contextual use, secure engagement, digital identity management, and basic purpose-environment knowledge. The total Cronbach α value of the scale is .980; For the "awareness" subscale, which consists of 17 items. 968; .958 for the 9-item "contextual use" subscale; .928 for the 6-item "safe participation" subscale; It was calculated as .908 for the "digital identity management" subscale consisting of 4 items and .899 for the "basic tool and environment knowledge" subscale consisting of 5 items. In this context, it is possible to accept both the whole and the subscales of the scale as highly reliable (Acar, 2015).

The Toronto Alexithymia Scale is a 20-item likert-type scale scored between 1–5 and the Turkish version developed by Bagby et al. was made by Sayar et al. in

2001. High scores from the scale, which has three sub-dimensions: difficulty recognizing emotions, difficulty in expressing emotions and extroverted thinking, indicate a high level of alexithymia (Aydın et al., 2013).

The revised Cyberbullying Inventory is the version of the Cyberbullying Inventory developed by Topçu and Erdur-Baker in 2007 and later revised. The scale consists of 14 items and consists of two subscales: exposure to cyberbullying and application of cyberbullying. The Cronbach α value of the scale is .920.

The validity and reliability study of the "Cyber-Violence Legitimation Scale," which consists of 16 questions aimed at legitimizing violence and cyber-violence, was also conducted by the researcher and its alpha value was determined as .752.

9. DESCRIPTIVE STATISTICS

9.1. Demographic Information

Between June and September 2016, 400 university students participated in the research on a voluntary basis. When Table 1 is examined, the distribution of the students participating in the research according to their gender is seen. Accordingly, 51.5 % (n = 206) of the 400 university students participating in the study were female and 48.5 % (n = 194) were male.

It is possible to say that the distribution of participants on the basis of age variable ranged from 18 to 25 and that the most participants from the age group of 20 (29 %; n = 116) took part in the study (Table 2).

Table 1: Gender

	N	%
Female	206	51.5
Male	194	48.5
Total	400	100.0

Table 2: Age

	N	%
18,00	29	7.2
19,00	65	16.3
20,00	116	29.0
21,00	77	19.3
22,00	60	15.0
23,00	27	6.8
24,00	22	5.5
25,00	4	1.1
Total	400	100.0

In Tables 3 and 4, the distribution of the participants according to the universities and faculties they studied is given. It is seen that the highest participation is as follows: Maltepe University (23 %); Gelişim University (22 %); Bahçeşehir University (20 %); Yıldız Technical University (20 %); Istanbul Technical

University (7.5 %) and Marmara University (7.5 %). The ranking of the faculties with participation from universities is as follows: Faculty of Health Sciences (25.5 %); Vocational School (21.2 %); Faculty of Engineering (74 %); Faculty of Economics and Administrative Sciences (9.2 %); Faculty of Communication (7.1 %); Faculty of Educational Sciences (6.7 %); Faculty of Law (4 %); Faculty of Architecture and Design (3.8 %); Faculty of Arts and Sciences (3.5 %) and Faculty of Medicine (1.8 %).

Table 3: Universities that Participants Study

	N	%
Bahçeşehir University	80	20.0
İstanbul Technical University	30	7.5
Yıldız Technical University	80	20,0
Maltepe University	92	23.0
Gelişim University	88	22.0
Marmara University	30	7.5
Total	400	100.0

Table 4: Departments of Participants

	N	%
Vocational School	84	21.2
Engineering	74	18.4
Educational Sciences	27	6.7
Faculty of Art	14	3.5
Law	16	4
	15	3.8
Communication Faculty	28	7.1
Business School	35	9.2
Health Faculty	100	25.5
Medicine	7	1.8
Total	400	100.0

9.2. Social Media Usage Habits

The social media usage habits of the university students participating in the research were examined under three different headings.

The majority of the participants shared photos 1–2 times daily on social media (Table 5; 48.6 %), the majority of them shared videos 1–2 times on social media daily (Table 6; 31.0 %), and the most common types of sharing (Table 7) were found as personal photos (83.8 %), funny-entertainment-humor (35.3 %), news (18.8 %), politics (17.5 %), scientific articles (15.5 %), columns/journalists' articles (12.5 %) and music videos (11.5 %). In the light of these findings, it is possible to say that research participants actively use social media. It is seen that the sample group of the research is pathological or not very intensely active in social media. This allowed participants to be considered as "average" users. Since it is thought that the answers of users who use social media intensively or pathologically or who are addicted to the internet may be biased, the sample group was ensured to remain more homogeneous.

Table 5: Sharing Photograph

	N	%
Never	21	6.1
Rare	25	7.2
0–1 times	71	16.6
1–2 times	199	48.6
2–3 times	60	14.1
3–4 times	24	7.4
Total	400	100

Table 6: Video Sharing

	N	%
	106	26.5
Rare	17	4.3
0–1 times	61	15.3
1–2 times	124	31.0
2–3 times	69	17.3
3–4 times	23	5.8
Total	400	100

Table 7: Social Media Sharing Habits

	N	%
Kişisel Fotoğraflar	335	83.8
Komik- Eğlence-Mizah	141	35.3
Haber	75	18.8
Siyaset	70	17.5
Bilimsel Yazılar	62	15.5
Köşe Yazıları/ Gazetecilerin Yazıları	50	12.5
Müzik Videoları	46	11.5

9.3. Inferential Statistics

The validity and reliability study of the "Cyber-Violence Justification Scale," which consists of 16 questions aimed at legitimizing violence and cyber-violence, was also conducted by the researcher and its alpha value was determined as .752. In the process of developing the scale, 20 questions were prepared to evaluate the attitudes and perceptions of the participants toward legitimizing violence and the scale was applied with university students consisting of 50 people in June. In order to measure whether the pilot application of 50 people is sufficient for factor analysis and reliability tests, it is necessary to first perform sampling proficiency statistics (Kaiser-Mayer-Olkin, KMO) and Bartlett Globality Test. The prerequisite for performing factor analysis is that there is a certain correlation between the variables. The Bartlett globality test shows whether there is enough relationship between the variables. If the p value of the Bartlett test is lower than 0.05 significance, there is a sufficient relationship between the variables to perform factor analysis (Durmuş et al., 2011: 79). When Table 1 was examined, it was shown that the p value was less than 0.05 and that the sample was sufficient and related to perform factor analysis.

Table 8: KMO & Bartlett's Test

KMO & Bartlett's Test		
Kaiser-Meyer-Olkin Measure of Sampling Adequacy.		.467
Bartlett's Test of Sphericity	Approx. Chi-Square	359.369
	df	190
	Sig.	**.000**

After the factor analysis, it was found that the 20-question scale of justification of violence was a 7-factor structure that explained 70.5 % of the total variance (Table 9).

Table 9: Factor Analysis

Component	Initial Eigenvalues			Extraction Sums of Squared Loadings		
	Total	% of Variance	Cumulative %	Total	% of Variance	Cumulative %
1	3,720	18,600	18,600	3,720	18,600	18,600
2	3,142	15,708	34,308	3,142	15,708	34,308
3	1,801	9,006	43,315	1,801	9,006	43,315
4	1,567	7,834	51,149	1,567	7,834	51,149
5	1,521	7,606	58,755	1,521	7,606	58,755
6	1,291	6,454	65,209	1,291	6,454	65,209
7	1,068	5,342	70,551	1,068	5,342	70,551
8	.844	4,222	74,773			
9	.751	3,756	78,529			
10	.714	3,569	82,098			
11	.695	3,476	85,574			
12	.649	3,245	88,819			
13	.520	2,602	91,421			
14	.374	1,870	93,291			
15	.332	1,658	94,949			
16	.306	1,528	96,477			
17	.237	1,186	97,663			
18	.220	1,098	98,761			
19	.182	.911	99,672			
20	.066	.328	100,000			

Extraction Method: Principal Component Analysis.

After the factor analysis, the reliability study of the scale was performed. In the first reliability analysis, the alpha value was determined as .692, but when the 1st, 11th, 15th and 16th questions were removed, it was determined that the reliability coefficient of the scale was .752 and it was decided to design the scale to consist of 16 items by considering it appropriate by the researcher to remove these questions (Table 10).

Table 10: Reliability Analysis of Cyber-Violence Justification Scale

Cronbach's Alpha	Cronbach's Alpha Based on Standardized Items	N of Items
.752	.760	16

After the reliability analyzes, the factor analysis of the scale was performed again and finally a reliable (α = .752) and 3-factor structure of 16 items was reached. This 3-factor structure explains 50 % of the total variance (Table 11). However, although a three-dimensional structure emerged in the factor analysis, since cyber-violence is considered to be a holistic phenomenon, the measurement was made holistically, and the scale was evaluated as one-dimensional.

Table 11: The Last Factor Analysis Of Justification of Cyber-Violence Scale

Component	Initial Eigenvalues			Rotation Sums of Squared Loadings		
	Total	% of Variance	Cumulative %	Total	% of Variance	Cumulative %
1	3,590	22,439	22,439	3,144	19,651	19,651
2	2,883	18,021	40,460	3,046	19,037	38,688
3	1,603	10,018	50,478	1,886	11,790	50,478
4	1,316	8,222	58,701			
5	1,163	7,266	65,967			
6	.948	5,925	71,891			
7	.795	4,968	76,860			
8	.703	4,394	81,254			
9	.622	3,885	85,139			
10	.576	3,599	88,738			
11	.494	3,090	91,828			
12	.403	2,516	94,344			
13	.299	1,870	96,214			
14	.278	1,737	97,951			
15	.217	1,357	99,308			
16	.111	.692	100,000			

Extraction Method: Principal Component Analysis.

10. RELATIONAL ANALYSIS

Table 12: Relationship Between Digital Media Literacy and Alexithymia

		Digital Media Literacy	Alexithymia
Digital Media Literacy	Pearson Correlation	1	-.218**
	Sig. (2-tailed)		.000
	N	400	399
Alexithymia	Pearson Correlation	-.218**	1
	Sig. (2-tailed)	.000	
	N	399	399

**. Correlation is significant at the 0.01 level (2-tailed).

1. Is there a significant relationship between information literacy and alexithymia?

   H0 = There is no significant relationship between information literacy and alexithymia.

   H1 = There is a significant relationship between information literacy and alexithymia.

When the correlation between information literacy and alexithymia is examined (Table 12), it is seen that the p value is 0.000. Since the p value is less than 0.05, H0 is rejected and H1 is accepted. In this context, a significant difference was found between information literacy and alexithymia.

Table 13: Relationship Between Alexithymia and Justification of Cyber-Violence

		Alexithyymia	Justification of Cyber-Violence
Alexithymia	Pearson Correlation	1	.144**
	Sig. (2-tailed)		.004
	N	400	400
Justification of	Pearson Correlation	.144**	1
Cyber-Violence	Sig. (2-tailed)	.004	
	N	399	400

**. Correlation is significant at the 0.01 level (2-tailed).

2. Is there a significant relationship between justification of cyber-violence and alexithymia?

H0 = There is no significant relationship between justification of cyber-violence and alexithymia?

H1 = There is a significant relationship between justification of cyber-violence and alexithymia?

When the correlation between justification of cyber-violence and alexithymia (Table 13) is examined, it is seen that the p value is 0.004. Since the P value is less than 0.05, H0 is rejected and H1 is accepted. Therefore, a significant difference was found between justification of cyber-violence and alexithymia.

Table 14: Relationship Between Justification of Cyber-Violence and Cyber-Victimization

		Justification of Cyber-Violence	Cyber-Victimization
Justification of	Pearson	1	.109*
Cyber-Violence	Correlation		
	Sig. (2-tailed)		.029
	N	400	400
Cyber-Victimization	Pearson	.109*	1
	Correlation		
	Sig. (2-tailed)	.029	
	N	400	400

*. Correlation is significant at the 0.05 level (2-tailed).

3. Is there a significant relationship between justification of cyber-violence and cyber-victimization?

HO = There is no significant relationship between the justification of cyber-violence and cyber-victimization?

H1 = There is a significant relationship between the justification of cyber-violence and cyber-victimization?

When the correlation between the justification of cyber-violence and cyber-victimization is examined (Table 14), it is seen that the p value is 0.029. Since the p value is less than 0.05, HO is rejected and H1 is accepted. So, there is a significant difference between justification of cyber-violence and cyber-victimization.

Table 15: Relationship Between Justification of Cyber-Violence and Cyberbullying

		Justification of Cyber-Violence	Cyberbullying
Justification of Cyber-Violence	Pearson Correlation	1	.144**
	Sig. (2-tailed)		.004
	N	400	400
Cyberbullying	Pearson Correlation	.144**	1
	Sig. (2-tailed)	.004	
	N	400	400

**. Correlation is significant at the 0.01 level (2-tailed).

4. Is there a significant relationship between the justification of cyber-violence and cyberbullying?

HO = There is no significant relationship between the justification of cyber-violence and cyberbullying?

H1 = There is a significant relationship between the justification of cyber-violence and cyberbullying?

When the correlation between the justification of cyber-violence and cyber-bullying is examined (Table 15), it is seen that the p value is 0.004. Since the p value is less than 0.05, HO is rejected and H1 is accepted. In this context, a significant difference was found between the justification of cyber-violence and cyberbullying.

Table 16: Relationship Between Justification of Cyber-Violence and Digital Media Literacy

		Justification of Cyber-Violence	Digital Media Literacy
Justification of Cyber-Violence	Pearson Correlation	1	.041
	Sig. (2-tailed)		**.408**
	N	400	400
Digital Media Literacy	Pearson Correlation	.041	1
	Sig. (2-tailed)	**.408**	
	N	400	400

5. Is there a significant relationship between the justification of cyber-violence and digital media literacy?

H0 = There is no significant relationship between the justification of cyber-violence and digital media literacy?

H1 = There is a significant relationship between the justification of cyber-violence and digital media literacy?

When the correlation between the justification of cyber-violence and digital media literacy is examined (Table 16), it is seen that the p value is 0.408. Since the p value is greater than 0.05, H1 is rejected and H0 is accepted. Therefore, there is no significant difference between justification of cyber-violence and digital media literacy.

Table 17: Relationship Between Cyber-Victimization and Alexithymia

		Cyber-Victimization	Alexithymia
Cyber-victimization	Pearson Correlation	1	**.233****
	Sig. (2-tailed)		**.000**
	N	400	399
Alexithymia	Pearson Correlation	**.233****	1
	Sig. (2-tailed)	**.000**	
	N	399	399

**. Correlation is significant at the 0.01 level (2-tailed).

6. Is there a significant relationship between cyber-victimization and alexithymia?

H0 = There is no significant relationship between cyber-victimization and alexithymia.

H1 = There is a significant relationship between cyber-victimization and alexithymia.

When the correlation between cyber-victimization and alexithymia is examined (Table 17), it is seen that the p value is 0.000. Since the p value is less than 0.05, H0 is rejected and H1 is accepted. Therefore, a significant difference was found between cyber-victimization and alexithymia.

Table 18: Relationship Between Cyberbullying and Alexithymia

		Cyberbullying	Alexithymia
Cyberbullying	Pearson Correlation	1	-.127*
	Sig. (2-tailed)		.011
	N	400	399
Alexithymia	Pearson Correlation	-.127*	1
	Sig. (2-tailed)	.011	
	N	399	399

*. Correlation is significant at the 0.05 level (2-tailed).

7. Is there a significant relationship between cyberbullying and alexithymia?

H0 = There is no significant relationship between cyberbullying and alexithymia.

H1 = There is a significant relationship between cyberbullying and alexithymia.

When the correlation between exhibiting cyberbullying behavior and alexithymia is examined (Table 18), it is seen that the p value is 0.011. Since the p value is less than 0.05, H0 is rejected and H1 is accepted. In this context, a significant difference was found between cyberbullying and alexithymia.

Table 19: Relationship Between Cyberbullying and Digital Media Literacy

		Cyberbullying	Digital Media Literacy
Cyberbullying	Pearson Correlation	1	-.008
	Sig. (2-tailed)		.876
	N	400	400
Digital Media Literacy	Pearson Correlation	-.008	1
	Sig. (2-tailed)	.876	
	N	400	400

8. Is there a significant relationship between cyberbullying and digital media literacy?

H0 = There is no significant relationship between cyberbullying and digital media literacy.

H1 = There is a significant relationship between cyberbullying and digital media literacy.

When the correlation between cyberbullying behavior and digital media literacy is examined (Table 19), it is seen that the p value is 0.876. Since the p value is greater than 0.05, H1 is rejected and H0 is accepted. In this context, there is no significant difference between cyberbullying and digital media literacy.

Table 20: Relationship Between Cyber-Victimization and Digital Media Literacy

		Digital Media Literacy	Cyber-Victimization
Digital Media Literacy	Pearson Correlation	1	-.081
	Sig. (2-tailed)		.107
	N	400	400
Cyber-Victimization	Pearson Correlation	-.081	1
	Sig. (2-tailed)	.107	
	N	400	400

9. Is there a significant relationship between cyber-victimization and digital media literacy?

H0 = There is no significant relationship between cyber-victimization and digital media literacy.

H1 = There is a significant relationship between cyber-victimization and digital media literacy.

When the correlation between cyber-victimization and digital media literacy is examined (Table 20), it is seen that the p value is 0.107. Since the p value is greater than 0.05, H1 is rejected and H0 is accepted. So, there is no significant difference between cyber-victimization and digital media literacy.

Table 21: Relationship Between Cyber-Victimization and Cyberbullying

		Cyber-Victimization	Cyberbullying
Cyber-Victimization	Pearson Correlation	1	.628**
	Sig. (2-tailed)		.000
	N	400	400
Cyberbullying	Pearson Correlation	.628**	1
	Sig. (2-tailed)	.000	
	N	400	400

**. Correlation is significant at the 0.01 level (2-tailed).

10. Is there a signifigant relationship between being cyber-victimization and cyberbullying?

H0 = There is no significant relationship between cyber-victimization and cyberbullying?

H1 = There is a significant relationship between being cyber-victimization and cyberbullying?

When we examined the correlation between cyber-victimization and cyberbullying (Table 21), the p value is 0.000. Since the p value is less than 0.05, H0 is rejected and H1 is accepted. Therefore, a significant difference was found between cyber-victimization and cyberbullying.

11. RESULTS

With the development of digital technology, especially the fact that the internet is seen as a second living place for individuals and has become an indispensable element of daily life has the capacity to harm both for benefit and when not used consciously. The changes and developments in technology have not only changed the size of communication with the internet environment and social media, but also facilitated the lives of individuals and societies. However, it is also seen that unconscious uses trigger pathological conditions such as addiction, cyber-violence or practice, numbness by being exposed to intense elements of violence, depression, anxiety, anxiety, anxiety, stress if there is an individual intimacy, and even the inability to get satisfaction from one's own life by following the lives of others (stalking) on social media. In this context, being a conscious internet and social media user confronts researchers with both media literacy and digital media literacy.

The relationship between the media and violence, which is one of the main topics of this study, should be examined in terms of both violence and the media. The phenomenon of violence has been exhibited under different forms not only in the 21st century but also throughout the ages and has even been accepted at times. At this point, it becomes important that individuals and societies see violence as a normal situation or a strictly forbidden event at which border. When the effect of the media on shaping the thoughts, attitudes and beliefs of individuals and even their daily lives in the long term rather than in the short term is taken into consideration, the effect of violence elements in the media on the perceptions of violence of individuals emerges. Individual differences in people's perceptions of violence are taken into consideration, but in the light of the studies carried out, it is seen that intense media bombardment leads to numbness of people and not being able to give the natural, humane reactions they should. While numbness represents desensitization to any subject, alexithymia (emotional deafness) can be defined as not being aware of the individual's emotions, reacting differently than they should, or not giving them at all. Desensitized individuals come to the point of alexithymia after a while and after that they may make wrong decisions when evaluating or reacting to violence. Those who are the subject of this study can be summarized as seeing the use of violence as legitimate, justifying it and even seeing it as a right that people should use.

Unlike physical violence, cyber-violence is a type of violence carried out through social media, the internet or any information technology tool.

Considering that the borders between countries and cultures have been removed in the virtual environment with the internet, cyber-violence is considered as a global issue, not a local or national issue. Within the concept of cyber-violence, the "information pollution" on the internet and social media also raises the necessity of investigating which information is real and which is asparagus. Because the phenomenon of violence spreads very quickly, especially in social media, and finds a lot of supporters. That is why the concepts of violence in the media, violence in real life and cyber-violence are interrelated. Violence that is intensely exposed to in the media can be actively included in real life and in the virtual environment. Based on this idea, in the light of the information presented above and taking into account the results of the literature review, this research conducted with 400 university students continuing their university education in Istanbul.

First, the demographic characteristics of the research participants were examined. Accordingly, 51.5 % (206) of the participants were female and 48.5 % (194) were male. It is possible to say that the number of university students participating in the research is almost evenly distributed on the basis of genders.

When the age groups of the participants were examined, it was seen that it varied between the ages of 18 and 25 and that the most participants were in the 20 age group (29 %; N = 116).

The research participants were selected from a total of six universities, three states and three foundations continuing their university education in Istanbul, and attention was paid to the heterogeneity of the faculties they received education from. In this context, university students who continue their undergraduate education at Istanbul Technical University, Yıldız Technical University and Marmara University as state universities and Bahçeşehir University, Maltepe University and Gelişim University as foundation universities were included in the study.

When the social media usage habits of the participants were examined, it was determined that they preferred photo sharing over video sharing (48.6 %; 31 %). In social media shares, it was found that the participants preferred to share personal photos (83.8 %) the most, while they preferred music videos (11.5 %) relatively less than other categories. When the other categories were examined, it was determined that the participants were active social media users (funny-entertainment- humor 35.3 %; news 18.8 %; politics 17.5 %; scientific articles 15.5 %; columns/journalists' articles 12.5 %).

In the analyzes made within the scope of the research, the relationship between the variables was examined. First, a strong and negative relationship was found between information literacy and alexithymia. As adolescents' information literacy levels increase, their level of alexithymia decreases. This finding has been interpreted as increasing the awareness of adolescents of information literacy.

In the relationship analyzes, it was found that there was no relationship between information literacy and exposure to cyberbullying. Likewise, no significant relationship was found between exhibiting cyberbullying behavior and information literacy. While examining these findings of the research, adolescents evaluate themselves about information literacy and the importance given to information literacy in Turkey is taken into consideration. Especially considering that there is a different culture in social media, it has been interpreted as an understandable finding that information literacy has no direct effect. Although information literacy has been identified as a preventive factor for cyberbullying compared to studies in the literature (Buckingham, 2007; Hobbs, 2010) found that there was no relationship between digital media literacy and cyber-victimization and cyberbullying behavior.

Cyber-victimization meaningfully explains exhibiting cyberbullying behavior. Individuals who are exposed to cyberbullying are more prone to cyber-violence against others. In addition to many studies conducted in the literature, this finding was described as meaningful within the scope of the social learning model. According to the social learning model, individuals learn by taking models or imitating. Therefore, the individual who is exposed to violence may also inflict violence on other people (Erjem and Çağlayandereli, 2006). Therefore, this finding is consistent with many studies in the literature, with researchers stating that there is a strong relationship between exposure to cyberbullying and exhibiting this behavior (Kowalski and Limber, 2007; Li, 2007; Ybarra et al., 2012).

In general, when the results obtained from the research are listed; It has been found that the relationship between information literacy and alexithymia affects the legitimate view of cyber-violence. Information literacy alone does not affect exposure to cyberbullying and exhibiting cyberbullying behavior as a factor, but it does affect alexithymia along with these two variables. When the relationships of the variables with each other were examined, it was seen that there was a strong relationship between being exposed to cyberbullying and exhibiting cyberbullying behavior, and it was found that individuals exposed to cyberbullying were more likely to exhibit cyberbullying behavior. Again, according to the analyzes, alexithymia also affects the legitimacy of cyber-violence. In addition, exhibiting cyberbullying behavior has been found to be associated with alexithymia. There is also a significant relationship between information literacy and alexithymia. According to relationship analysis, cyber-violence is justified and cyberbullying; justification of cyber-violence and demonstrating cyberbullying behavior; while there was a significant relationship between alexithymia and exposure to cyber-bullying and exhibiting alexithymia and cyberbullying behavior; no significant relationship was found between digital media literacy and cyber-victimization and cyberbullying.

12. DISCUSSION

The concept of media and violence, which has an important place in media theories and research, and the effect of this concept on individuals is one of the frequently discussed topics. Although the debates were initially shaped through television violence, with the development of technology and especially the penetration of social media into the lives of individuals, the concept of media and violence began to be evaluated under headings such as violence over the internet, pornography, hate speech, video games. Within the scope of this study, the interaction and12 relationship between information literacy, exposure to cyber-violence and exhibiting this behavior, the levels of alexithymia of individuals and the legitimization of cyber-violence were examined in a conceptual framework and quantitative research was conducted to examine the variables for adolescents to legitimize cyber-violence.

Considering the point reached by science and interdisciplinary studies in the 21st century, the topic of media and violence is examined not only by communication theorists but also by sciences such as pedagogy, sociology, psychology, psychiatry and neurology in their studies such as the relationship between exposure to violent visuals and the study of decision-making mechanisms in the brain. In the 1950s, the debates around the argument that television causes violence began to take shape around the question of whether television causes violence or whether the tendency to violence in individuals is reflected on television.

Violence is a phenomenon that has emerged in different ways since human existence, sometimes accepted as the norm according to ages and sometimes applied by authority under the mask of "punishment." The existence of violence in the structure of man and society does not mean that it is a "right." However, being exposed to intense violence causes individuals to normalize violence and then see it as legitimate. At this point, it should be taken into consideration that violence in the media and violence in real life have the same effect on the perception of the individual. Researchers who set out from this information do not evaluate violence in the media and violence in real life independently of each other but examine the interaction between them.

Violence has an effect on the structure of individuals and societies; but short-term but frequent violence reveals that the person becomes desensitized after a while and cannot give the necessary reaction. At this point, the person has difficulties not only socially but also neurologically in making decisions, reacting or solving problems. The individual who accepts violence as normal in his / her individual life may see it as legitimate after a while. In this research, the legitimacy of violence was examined through information literacy, alexithymia, exposure to cyber-violence and the behavior of exhibiting cyber-violence. According to the results of the research, individuals' information literacy levels, alexithymia levels and exposure to cyberbullying have an effect on their legitimization of cyber-violence.

It is clear that the individual who legitimizes violence in his private life will also legitimize violence in society. As a momentary reaction, although the application of violence to the perpetrator of violence can be seen as a reasonable reaction, perceiving it as a "right" may cause individuals to approve violence more and to accept violence as one of the solutions that can be used.

In this study, the justification of cyber-violence was tried to be measured with questions such as "The death penalty can be applied for some crimes," "People who kill prisoners convicted of rape in prison should not be punished," "When sharing a news about violence on social media, I pay attention to whether the news is in the judicial process or not." The positive responses of the participants to such questions for the death penalty and their consideration of the judicial process in sharing news were associated with the concept of digital citizenship. Therefore, it is thought-provoking that the pictures of the criminals who have not yet been concluded or convicted, their names and surnames, and the cities they live in can be easily spread on social media. Because the cases of these people have not yet been concluded. The inability to be aware of digital citizenship is likewise considered in a wide range of ways, from publishing a photo of a friend on social media without permission to publishing personal information with false information. The point that needs to be considered here is that the victims of unconvicted cases are sentenced to a social punishment before a legal punishment. News that can spread very quickly through social media is similarly supported through campaigns on sites such as change.org and signatures are collected against people. In the cases against which a verdict has been rendered, it should not be forgotten that the persons sentenced to punishment as well as the victim have dignity and personality rights. All these are primary responsibilities of living in the rule of law. But the fine line here should not be forgotten again. Whether it is a victim or a perpetrator, while observing the personality rights of individuals, it should be taken into consideration that their actions are "crimes" and there should be a sanction. One of the findings of this research is that individuals who are cyberbullied are more likely to exhibit cyber violent behavior. Similar results are often seen in other studies in the literature. Because according to the theory of learning by modeling, people are more inclined to do the actions done to others. However, this does not mean that cyber-violence is normal or legitimate. It only demonstrates the need to reduce exposure to these behaviors in order to break the cycle of cyberbullying.

One of the other issues discussed in the relationship between media and violence is that the characters in the media are taken as an example by children and young people and their behaviors that are not accepted in social norms can be tolerated, justified and evaluated within a logical framework. For example, polygamy, which is not accepted socially, having illegitimate children, substance use or bullying is presented as an office to be envied, as well as forgetting that the characters of the series dealing with such topics are completely "fictional," and that their behaviors are often cited as a reason for their childhood traumas and poor environmental conditions are also important elements in legitimizing violence. As emphasized above, poor environmental conditions or childhood traumas can harm people's lives and put them in undesirable situations. But this should never be presented as a valid reason for committing violence. The extras of the violent elements in the media products are often presented as helpless, lonely, traumatized, and their actions are made innocent and, worse, placed on a legitimate basis. While conscious users can evaluate and analyze such fictional structures, it is seen that unconscious users accept these structures presented in the media as if they were "real" and "true" without questioning and analyzing them. Especially in childhood, children who are developmentally unable to distinguish between real and imaginary are negatively affected not only by the characters in cartoons or films, but also by the presentation of products in advertisements, perceiving the "supernatural" powers of the presented products as real. In addition to all these, long-term and intensely exposed to violent news, videos and images causes the individual to be emotionally deaf after a while and to be unable to react because he accepts the situation as normal. This is one of the obstacles in front of raising individuals who are aware of their conscious and civic responsibilities targeted by information literacy and media literacy. For this reason, it is necessary not only to reduce or control violence in the media, but also to raise conscious users, to increase the awareness of individuals about violence, and to emphasize that media products, especially the characters in the series, are fictional in information and media literacy trainings. In this context, Gerbner's "sowing theory" and General Aggression Model are guiding for researchers and professionals working in this field. Based on the data they obtained in the "Cultural Indicators Project," Gerbner and his team determined that stereotypical, repetitive thoughts, behaviors and role models presented on television were "cultivated" in the minds of individuals. As a result of their studies, they stated that not only violent images or behaviors, but also patterns such as gender roles, relations between men and women, problem-solving skills were included in the programs presented on television in a repetitive way and that individuals learned this. In this study, it was determined in this study that not only in people who are frequently exposed to social media and the internet, but also in average users, exposure to cyber-violence or exhibiting cyberbullying behavior causes individuals to reach the level of emotional deafness and to see cyber-violence as a legitimate right at a later level. Patterns and violent figures that take place on television in the form of patterns and repeaters are seen in social media in the form of cyber-violence and in a way that the individual is directly exposed to or exhibits. As determined in the findings of the study, taking part in such violent events was also determined to be related to the alexithymia levels of individuals.

In this research, it was seen that the measurements for the information literacy of individuals were mostly evaluated by the skills for the use of computer hardware and software, and the evaluations made within the framework of social life with the rights of the internet and social media in daily life such as "digital citizenship" were more limited. The use of information technology tools is important when evaluating information literacy, but the events that cause cyber-violence in the social sense are not the technical use of the computer, but the parts related to its social use. Therefore, it is thought that more awareness and awareness trainings should be given on issues such as personal rights and freedoms, harmful behaviors and hate speech as well as the technical features of computers and internet. In addition, it is thought that these studies should not be limited to children and young people, and that adult and elderly individuals should definitely benefit from these awareness and awareness raising activities. While all these studies are carried out, the subject should not be handled only as one-dimensional; It is thought that the joint work of communication, pedagogy, sociology, neurology and psychiatry sciences will be an important step in legitimizing cyber-violence.

Considering the people who are emotionally deaf by the intense and continuous violence, it is thought that it will be beneficial for both society and individuals to evaluate and present information and media literacy within the framework of the legitimacy of cyber-violence, especially for new generations.

CONCLUSION AND SUGGESTIONS

Online social networks encourage to establish the relationship among users of the networks globally. Traditionally online social networks are meant for keeping existing relationship and creating new relationships based on interests. But for this age online social networks are used as a rich set of the database for decision-making and as a medium for communication. For this reason, although there are benefits for those, some users can use online social networks for hate speech or online extremism. Those are not so big group, but their impact is more and harmful for victims. Moreover, especially hate speeches toward religion such as Islam, Hindu, Christian or Jews, due to those religion contains the group of people, the hate speech against this is more harmful than against an individual (Chetty and Alathur, 2018).

Victims of cyber-harassment believe that "I deserve it" and unfortunately, they internalize those hate speeches and harassment. Unfortunately, it could lead to justification of cyber-violence. In terms of violence toward "others" not only real presence of risk but also imagined and implied presence is important.

Countries and societies should develop common principles to improve overall social unity. Digital media literacy education and enhance individuals' digital citizenship skills. Moreover, especially for immigrants' justification cyber-violence, social cohesion is vital, and immigrants should be integrated to society. Add to this, countries should become social welfare state. In these countries individuals are not tend to discrimination or hate speech. But if the society become poorer and poverty is pervasive then hate speech, hate crime and justification of violence toward immigrants become pervasive. All these factors are linked to each other.

APPENDIXES

APPENDICES

APPENDIX 1 PERSONAL INFORMATION

Gender:
Age:
Department:
How many photos do you share on social media on a daily basis?
……………………………………………………………………………..

How many videos do you share on social media on a daily basis?
……………………………………………………………………………..

What kind of sharing do you do in general?
(a) Personal photos (b) Funny- fun- humor (c) News (d) Politics (e) Scientific articles (f) Columnists- journalists' articles (g) Music videos

APPENDIX 2 DIGITAL MEDIA LITERACY SCALE

1: Not Enough at All; 2: Less Enough; 3: Medium Enough; 4: Too Much; 5: Fully Adequate

	1	2	3	4	5
1. Ability to eliminate simple problems encountered in the digital tools used					
2. Ability to transfer files from one to another of the media such as USB, DVD, external disk					
3. To know what hardware and software do in digital technologies					
4. To know what kind of hardware and software is needed to connect to the Internet					
5. Ability to choose digital tools that suit their needs and conditions					
6. Ability to choose an Internet Service Provider in accordance with their own expectations and conditions					
7. Ability to perform online transactions such as school, hospital, banking services and hotel reservations online					

	1	2	3	4	5
8. To be able to send electronic mail using internet-connected tools and to open incoming electronic mail					
9. To attach a file to the e-mail to be sent and to open the file attached to the incoming e-mail					
10. Ability to use at least one word processing software (such as Word, WordPad)					
11. Ability to use at least one spreadsheet software (such as Excel)					
12. Can use at least one presentation preparation software (such as PowerPoint)					
13. To be able to download and copy the audio, text or picture type content they need from the internet to the computer					
14. Ability to print out a document saved on the computer					
15. Ability to use search options when searching in search engines and databases					
16. In addition to online information sources, taking care to benefit from printed sources such as books, magazines, newspapers					

	1	2	3	4	5
17. To be able to evaluate the usefulness of information in digital environments in terms of its own purpose					
18. To be able to act critically and cautiously when using information in digital environment					
19. Know the risks that may arise in social networks, sharing sites and online communities					
20. Using online environments for communication, socialization and cooperation in a way that does not reduce face-to-face communication with other people					
21. To know that digital media provides more up-to-date information about social developments in the world than printed media					
22. To be able to recognize the messages or contents that they encounter in digital environments and whose main purpose is to create advertising or impact					
23. To be able to make sense of the message or content presented in digital environments without being affected by the presentation style of the presenter or organizations					
24. Caring that individuals are given at least a basic level of education in order to protect them from possible damages that may come from their digital environment					

	1	2	3	4	5
25. Seeing the use of digital environments as an indicator of democratic life and active citizenship					
26. To know the importance of digital environments in the shaping of the individual's worldview, values and habits					
27. To be aware that digital environments can make significant contributions to the lifelong learning of the individual					
28. Acting ethically and responsibly while sharing information through digital media					
29. When using the content in digital media, acting in accordance with the intellectual and legal rights of the content owners					
30. Be able to actively participate in at least one of the digital media such as social networks, forums, communities and sharing sites					
31. Ability to share information, documents, files in at least one of the digital media such as social networks, forums, communities and sharing sites					
32. To act in accordance with the legal and social rules applicable to the activities carried out in digital environments					

	1	2	3	4	5
33. To have an idea about the possible consequences of not complying with the applicable legal and social rules in digital environments					
34. Ability to make the privacy and security settings of any internet browser as it sees fit.					
35. When using digital tools, taking security measures such as creating user passwords, using virus protection software					
36. To be able to recognize situations such as online attacks, virus infections and theft of credentials when using digital media					
37. Not to leave private information in the digital environments that he/she browses, which can be later determined by others and used against him/herself.					
38. To be able to distinguish between personal information that is inconvenient to share with others in digital environments and that is not harmful to share					
39. To know the individual, legal and social consequences of actions such as online attacks and identity theft in digital environments					
40. To be able to evaluate the importance of the privacy policies of the websites used by the user for himself					

APPENDIX 3 REVISED CYBERBULLYING INVENTORY-RCBI

	I DID				SOMEONE DID TO ME			
	Never	1 times	2–3 times	More than 3	Never	1 times	2–3 times	More than 3
1. Retrieve information (files, photos, messenger conversation recordings, etc.) from the personal computer without permission								
2. Using an Internet nickname (nick) without permission								
3. Threatening in the chat room								
4. Insulting in the chat room								
5. Blocking access to social media accounts for no reason								
6. Disseminate information shared in Messenger to others without permission								
7. To make others watch while making private calls via webcam								
8. Making fun of comments and information posted on a forum site								

	I DID				SOMEONE DID TO ME			
	Never	1 times	2–3 times	More than 3	Never	1 times	2–3 times	More than 3
9. If the forum official (moderator or admin) cancels the membership for no reason								
10. Sending threatening, embarrassing, hurtful messages via e-mail								
11. Blocking access by obtaining passwords for e-mail accounts								
12. Accessing messages by obtaining the passwords of electronic mail accounts								
13. Sending threatening, embarrassing, hurtful messages via SMS								
14. Deceiving the other party by showing gender differently								

APPENDIX 4 TAÖ-20 TORONTO ALEXITHYMIA SCALE

Please mark the extent to which the following items describe you.
Rate these items as: Never (1),..............., Always (5)

	Never	Rarely	Sometimes	Often	Always
1. I often don't know exactly what I'm feeling	1	2	3	4	5
2. Finding the appropriate words for my feelings is hard for me	1	2	3	4	5
3. I have feelings in my body that even doctors do not understand	1	2	3	4	5
4. I can easily describe my feelings	1	2	3	4	5
5. I would rather solve problems than just describe them	1	2	3	4	5
6. When I'm in a bad mood, I don't know if I'm sad, scared, or angry	1	2	3	4	5
7. The sensations in my body confuse me	1	2	3	4	5
8. I prefer to leave things to their own devices, without trying to understand why it turned out the way	1	2	3	4	5
9. I have feelings that I can't fully identify	1	2	3	4	5
10. People need to recognize their feelings	1	2	3	4	5
11. It's hard for me to describe how I feel about people	1	2	3	4	5
12. People want me to describe my emotions easily	1	2	3	45	
13. I don't know what's going on inside of me	1	2	3	4	5
14. Most of the time I don't know why I'm angry	1	2	3	4	5

	Never	Rarely	Sometimes	Often	Always
15. I prefer to talk to people more about their daily pursuits than their feelings	1	2	3	4	5
16. I prefer to watch entertaining programs instead of psychological dramas	1	2	3	4	5
17. It is difficult for me to explain my inner feelings even to my close friends	1	2	3	4	5
18. Even in moments of silence, I can feel close to someone	1	2	3	4	5
19. I find it harmful to examine my emotions while solving my personal problems	1	2	3	4	5
20. Searching for hidden meanings in movies or games reduces the pleasure to be taken from them	1	2	3	4	5

APPENDIX 5 JUSTIFICATION OF CYBER-VIOLENCE SCALE

The following questions have been asked within the scope of an academic study and will not be published anywhere except for the scientific study and will not be shared with 3rd parties.

1: Strongly agree; 2: Agree; 3: Neither agree nor disagree; 4: Disagree; 5: Strongly disagree

1. In some cases, it could be acceptable that violence can be applied	1	2	3	4	5
2. I give back to the one who physically abuses me	1	2	3	4	5
3. The death penalty may be imposed for some crimes	1	2	3	4	5
4. Perpetrators of violence are punished that they legally deserve	1	2	3	4	5
5. Victims of violence should seek their rights through legal ways	1	2	3	4	5
6. It is the right of women who are victims of violence to inflict violence on the person who inflicts violence on them	1	2	3	4	5
7. It is the right of men who are victims of violence to inflict violence on the person who inflicts violence on them	1	2	3	4	5
8. People who kill prisoners convicted of rape in prison should not be punished	1	2	3	4	5
9. I respond to insults about my values (religion, language, sect, etc.) on social media with the same style	1	2	3	4	5
10. Sometimes people are insulted on social media because they deserve it	1	2	3	4	5
11. I do not need permission to share photos of my friends on social media	1	2	3	4	5
12. Membership in discussion groups on social media may be revoked if necessary	1	2	3	4	5

13. When sharing a news about violence on social media, I pay attention to the fact that there are no photographs of people related to the incident	1	2	3	4	5
14. When sharing a news about violence on social media, I pay attention that people related to the incident do not have personal information	1	2	3	4	5
15. When I share a post about violence on the social media, I pay attention to whether the news is in the judicial process or not	1	2	3	4	5
16. When sharing a post on social media, I pay attention that there are no hurtful statements	1	2	3	4	5

REFERENCES

Acar, Çiğdem. "Anne ve Babaların İlkokul, Ortaokul ve Lise Öğrencisi Çocukları İle Kendilerinin Dijital Okuryazarlıklarına İlişkin Görüşleri," Yayımlanmamış Yüksek Lisans Tezi. Ankara Üniversitesi EBE, 2015.

Akça, G. ve Başer, D. "'Karanlığın Yok Oluşu' Gelişen Teknolojinin Gizlilik ve Mahremiyet Üzerindeki Etkileri," Muğla Üniversitesi Sosyal Bilimler Enstitüsü Dergisi, Vol. 26, 2011, pp. 19–42.

Akın, İrem. "Relationship of Problematic Internet Use with Alexithymia, Emotion Regulation and Impulsivity," Yayınlanmamış Yüksek Lisans Tezi. Bahçeşehir Üniversitesi SBE, 2014.

Akkanat, Salih. "Şiddet ve İktidar: Şiddetin 'Meşruiyet'inden 'Meşruiyet'in Şiddetine," Yayımlanmamış Doktora Tezi. Marmara Üniversitesi SBE, 2011.

Allen Johnie J. ve Craig A. Anderson. "The General Aggression Model." In P. Roessler, C. Hoffner, L. van Zoonen ve N. Podschuweit (Eds.) International Encylopedia of Media Effects. Wiley-Blackwell, New Jersey, 2015.

Anderson Craig A. ve Brad J. Bushman. "Human Aggression," Annual Review of Psychology, Vol. 53, No. 1, 2002, pp. 27–51.

Anderson Craig A., Leonard Berkowitz, Edward Donnerstein, L. Rowell Huesmann, James D. Johnson, Daniel Linz, Neil M. Malamuth ve Ellen Wartella. "The Influence of Media Violence on Youth," Psychological Science in the Public Interest, Vol. 4, No. 3, 2003, pp. 81–110.

Anık, C. "EKONOMİ POLİTİK VE MEDYATİK ÜRÜN," Ankara

Ang Rebecca P. ve Dion H. Goh. "Cyberbullying Among Adolescents: The Role of Affective and Cognitive Empathy and Gender," Child Psychiatry Hum Dev, Vol. 41, 2010, pp. 387–397.

Arendt, H. "The Banality of Evil," Metis Press, İstanbul, 2016.

Aricak, O. T., & Ozbay, A. "Investigation of the relationship between cyberbullying, cybervictimization, alexithymia and anger expression styles among adolescents," Computers in Human Behavior, Vol. 55, 2016, pp. 278–285.

Avcı Özlem. "Dijital Yaşamın Dijital Özneleri: Herkes ya da Hiç Kimse," Uşak Üniversitesi Sosyal Bilimler Dergisi, Vol. 8, No. 1, 2015, pp. 249–266.

Aybek, Birsel ve Remzi Demir. "Lise Öğrencilerinin Medya ve Televizyon Okuryazarlık Düzeyleri İle Eleştirel Düşünme Eğilimlerinin İncelenmesi," Ç.Ü. Sosyal Bilimler Enstitüsü Dergisi, Vol. 22, No. 2, 2013, pp. 287–304.

Aydın Adem, Yavuz Selvi ve Pınar G. Özdemir, "Depresyon Hastalarında Aleksitiminin Bedenselleştirme ve Uyku Kalitesi Üzerine Etkisi," Nöropsikiyatri Arşivi Dergisi, Vol. 50, 2013, pp. 65-69.

Aydogan, D., & Buyukyilmaz, O. "The effect of social media usage on students' stress and anxiety: A Research in Karabuk University Faculty of Business," International Journal of Multidisciplinary Thought, Vol. 6, No.1, 2017, pp. 253-260.

Bacaksız, Tülin. "Medya Okuryazarlığı Dersinde Gazete ve Dergi Kullanımı: İzmir'de Medya Okuryazarlığı Dersinin Öğrencilerin Gazete ve Dergi Okuma Alışkanlıkları Üzerine Etkisi," Yayımlanmamış Yüksek Lisans Tezi. Gazi Üniversitesi Sosyal Bilimler Enstitüsü, 2010.

Bağlı Melike Türkan. "Medya Okuryazarlığı Hareketinde Yedi Büyük Tartışma," Ankara Üniversitesi Eğitim Bilimleri Fakülte Dergisi, Vol. 37, No. 1, 2004, pp. 122-140.

Bal, Enes. "Teknoloji Çağında Cep Telefonu Kullanım Alışkanlıkları ve Motivasyonlar: Selçuk Üniversitesi Öğrencileri Üzerine Bir İnceleme," Yayımlanmamış Doktora Tezi. Selçuk Üniversitesi Sosyal Bilimler Enstitüsü, 2013.

Bartholow Bruce D., Brad J. Bushman ve Marc A. Sestir. "Chronic Violent Game Exposure and Desensitization to Violence: Behavioral and Event-Related Brain Potential Data," Journal of Experimental Social Psychology, Vol. 42, 2006, pp. 532-539.

Barak Azy, Meyran Boniel-Nissim ve John Suler. "Fostering Empowerment in Online Support Groups," Computers in Human Behavior, Vol. 24, 2008, pp. 1867-1883.

Baran Aylin Görgün, Birsen Şahin Kütük ve Dicle Maybek. "Kadınların Eşleri Tarafından Gördükleri Şiddeti Meşrulaştırmaları Üzerinde Kamusal Alanın Etkisi," Sosyal ve Beşeri Bilimler Dergisi, Vol. 4, No. 2, 2012, pp. 41-50.

Barone Diane ve Todd E. Wright. "Literacy Instruction with Digital and Media Technologies," The Reading Teacher, Vol. 62, No. 4, 2008, pp. 292-302.

Bauman Sheri ve Heather Pero. "Bullying and Cyberbullying Among Deaf Students and Their Hearing Peers: An Exploratory Study," Journalof Deaf Studies and Deaf Education, Vol. 20, 2010, pp. 1-18.

Bayraktaroğlu Ali M. ve Berrin Bayraktaroğlu, B. "Gazetelerde Yer Alan Haber Fotoğraflarında Kötünün Sunumu Üzerine Bir İnceleme," Süleyman Demirel Üniversitesi Güzel Sanatlar Fakültesi Hakemli Dergisi, Vol. 4, 2009, pp. 1-25.

Baytun İnci Duygun ve Ayşen Özerem. "Teknolojik Determinizm Kavramı Kıskacında Eğitim," International Journal of New Trends in Arts, Sports & Science Education, Vol. 1, No. 4, 2012, pp. 45-53.

Bekker Maria H.J., Nathan Bachrach ve Marcel S. Croon. "The Relationships of Antisocial Behavior with Attachment Styles, Autonomy—Connectedness and Alexithymia," Journal of Clinical Psychology, Vol. 63, No. 6, 2007, pp. 507–527.

Benedikter Roland ve Nicholas Fitz. "Technophilia and the New Media: Contemporary Questions of Responsible Cultural Consumption, a Call for Public Debate," Synesis: A Journal of Science, Technology, Ethics and Policy, Vol. 2, 2011, pp. G62–G68.

Berson Ilene R. ve Michael J. Berson. "Challenging Online Behaviors of Youth: Findings from a Comparative Analysis of Young People in the United States and New Zealand," Social Science Computer Review, Vol. 23, No. 1, 2005, pp. 29–38.

Bhattacharya Haimanti. "Mass Media Exposure and Attitude Towards Spousal Violence," The Social Science Journal, 2016. http://dx.doi.org/10.1016/j.sos cij.2016.02.011

Binark, M., Karataş, Ş., Çomu, T. ve Koca, E. "Türkiye'de Twitter'da Trol Kültürü," Toplum ve Bilim, Vol. 135, 2015, pp. 124–157.

Binark Mutlu ve Mine Gencel Bek. Eleştirel Medya Okuryazarlığı- Kuramsal Yaklaşımlar ve Uygulamalar, Kalkedon Yayınları: İstanbul, 2010.

Bjelajac, Ž., ve Filipović, A. "Specific Characteristics of Digital Violence and Digital Crime," Pravo-teorija i praksa, Vol. 38, No. 4, 2021, pp. 16–32.

Bowlby, J. "Güvenli bir dayanak," S. Güneri, Çev, İatanbul: Psikoterapi Enstitüsü Eğitim Yayınları, 2012.

Boyd, D. "It's complicated: The social lives of networked teens," Yale University Press, 2014.

Brown, J.D. "Mass Media Influences on Sexuality," The Journal of Sex Research, Vol. 39, No. 1, 2002, pp. 42–45.

Buckingham David. "Digital Media Literacies: Rethinking Media Education in the Age of the Internet," Research in Comparative and International Education, Vol. 2, No. 1, 2007, pp. 43–55.

Bulut Mesut. "Bir Sosyal Temsil Araştırması: Medyada ve Üniversite Öğrencilerinde Törenin Algılanışı," Ç.Ü. Sosyal Bilimler Enstitüsü Dergisi, Vol. 17, No. 3, 2008, pp. 63–78.

Bushman Brad J. ve Craig A. Anderson. "Violent Video Games and Hostile Expectations: A Test of the General Aggression Model," Personality and Social Psychology Bulletin, Vol. 28, No. 12, 2002, pp. 1679–1686.

Bushman, B. J., & Huesmann, L. R. "Effects of violent media on aggression," Handbook of children and the media, 2012, pp. 231–248.

Calderón, C. A., de la Vega, G., & Herrero, D. B. "Topic modeling and characterization of hate speech against immigrants on Twitter around the emergence of a far-right party in Spain," Social Sciences, Vol. 9, No.11, 2020, pp. 188.

Cantor, J., & Riddle, K. "Media and fear in children and adolescents," Media violence and children: A complete guide for parents and professionals, 2014, pp. 179–207.

Carnagey Nicholas L., Craig A. Anderson ve Brad J. Bushman. "The Effect of Video Game Violence on Physiological Desensitization to Real-Lide Violence," Journal of Experimental Social Psychology, Vol. 43, 2007, pp. 489–496.

Catherina, Cappadocia M. "Cyberbullying and Cybervictimization: Prevalence, Stability, Risk and Protective Factors and Psychosocial Problems," York University, Master of Thesis, Toronto, 2008.

Croteau, D., Hoynes, W., & Milan, S. "Media society: Industries, Images, and Audiences," Second Edition, London, 2000.

Çalhan, Rabia. "Çocuğa Şiddetin Basında Sunumu (Cumhuriyet, Hürriyet ve Zaman Gazetelerinde Çocuk ve Şiddet Haberleri)," Yayınlanmamış Yüksek Lisans Tezi. Atatürk Üniversitesi Sosyal Bilimler Enstitüsü, 2008.

Çakır Hamza, Mustafa Koçer ve Hakan Aydın. "Medya Okuryazarlığı Dersini Alan ve Almayan İlköğretim Öğrencilerinin Medya İzleme Davranışlarındaki Farklılıkların Belirlenmesi," Selçuk İletişim Dergisi, Vol. 7, No. 3, 2012, pp. 43–54.

Çebi Murat Sadullah. "Gabriel Tarde'nin İzinde Medyanın İşlev ve Etkilerini Yeniden Gözden Geçirmek," İletişim Kuram ve Araştırma Dergisi, Vol. 36, 2013, pp. 1–28.

Çetinkaya, Selin. "Bilinçli Medya Kullanıcıları Yaratma Sürecinde Medya Okuryazarlığının Önemi," Yayınlanmamış Yüksek Lisans Tezi. Ankara Üniversitesi Sosyal Bilimler Enstitüsü, 2008.

Chang Fong-Ching, Chiu Chiung-Hui, Miao Nae-Fang, Chen Ping-Hung, Lee Ching-Mei, Huang Tzu-Fu ve Pan Yun-Chieh. "Online Gaming and Risks Predict Cyberbullying Perpetration and Victimization in Adolescent," International Journal of Public Health, Vol. 60, 2015, pp. 257–266.

Cheng John W., Hitoshi Mitomo, Tokio Otsuka ve Stefan Y. Jeon. "Cultivation Effects of Mass and Socail Media on Perceptions and Behavioural Intentions in Post-Disaster Recovery—The Case of the 2011 Great East Japan Earthquake," Telematics and Informatics, Vol. 33, 2016, pp. 753–772.

Christie, C., & Dill, E. "Evaluating peers in cyberspace: The impact of anonymity," Computers in Human Behavior, Vol. 55, 2016, pp. 292–299.

Chisholm June F. "Cyberspace Violence Against Girls and Adolescent Females," Annals New York Academy of Sciences, Vol. 1087, 2006, pp. 74–89.

Clayton Russell B. "The Third Wheel: The Impact of Twitter Use on Relationship Infidelity and Divorce," Cyberpsychology, Behavior and Social Networking, Vol. 17, No. 7, 2014, pp. 425–430.

Cranwell Jo, Kathy Whittamore, John Brinton ve Jo Leonardo-Bee. "Alcohol and Tobacco Content in UK Video Games and Their Association with Alcohol and Tobacco Use Among Young People," Cyberpsychology, Behavior and Social Networking, Vol. 19, No. 7, 2016, pp. 426– 434.

Cohen, Jonathan ve Gabriel Weimann. "Cultivation Revised: Some Genres Have Some Effects on Some Viewers," Communication Reports, Vol. 13, No. 2, 2000, pp. 99–114.

Corbett Patrick E. "Cyberbullying and Other High-Tech Crimes Involving Teens," Journal of Internet Law, Vol. 12, No. 3, 2008, pp. 12–20.

Coşkun, Berrak. "Hannah Arendt'te 'Radikal Kötülük' Problemi," Yayımlanmamış Yüksek Lisans Tezi. Maltepe Üniversitesi Sosyal Bilimler Enstitüsü, 2012.

Coşkun Yelkin Diker, Gonca Kızılkaya Cumaoğlu ve Hümset Seçkin. "Bilgisayar Öğretmen Adaylarının Bilişim Alanıyla İlgili Okuryazarlık Kavramlarına Yönelik Görüşleri," International Journal of Human Sciences, Vol. 10, No. 1, 2013, pp. 1259–1272.

Çomu, Tuğrul. "Video Paylaşım Ağlarında Nefret Söylemi: Youtube Örneği," Yayımlanmamış Yüksek Lisans Tezi. Ankara Üniversitesi Sosyal Bilimler Enstitüsü, 2012.

Çoklar, I., & Meşe, G. "Illinois Tecavüz Mitlerini Kabul Ölçeği Kısa Formunu Türkçe'ye Uyarlama Çalışması," Psikoloji Çalışmaları Dergisi, Vol. 34, No. 2, 2014, pp. 53–64.

Craparo Giuseppe, Alessio Gori, Irene Petruccelli, Vincenza Cannella ve Chiara Simonelli. "Intimate Partner Violence: Relationships Between Alexithimia, Depression, Attcahment Styles and Coping Strategies of Battered Women," The Journal of Sexual Medicine, Vol. 11, 2014, pp. 1484–1494.

Dănilă, I., Balazsi, R. ve Băban, A. "Pathways to Harsh Parenting: Testing a Social Information Processing Model of Child Abuse Using Meta-Analytic Structural Equation Modeling", Journal of Family Violence, Vol. 13, 2022, pp. 275–294. https://doi.org/10.1007/s10896-022-00428-z

Dal Nil Esra ve Veysel Dal. "Kişilik Özellikleri ve Sosyal Ağ Kullanım Alışkanlıkları: Üniversite Öğrencileri Üzerine Bir Araştırma," Mehmet Akif Ersoy Üniversitesi Sosyal Bilimler Enstitüsü Dergisi, Vol. 6, No. 11, 2014, pp. 144–162.

Daly John A. "Studying the Impacts of the Internet Without Assuming Technological Determinism," Aslib Proceedings, Vol. 52, No. 8, 2000, pp. 285–301.

DeFleur, M. L. "Mass communication theories, explaining origins, processes, and effect," Bostan: Pearson Education, 2010.

Deheu Francine, Catharine Bolman, Trıjntje Völlınk. "Cyberbullying: Youngsters' Experiences and Parental Perception," Cyberpsychology & Behavior, Vol. 11, No. 2, 2008, pp. 217–223.

Demirbaş Murat ve Rahmi Yağbasan. "Sosyal Öğrenme Teorisine Dayalı Öğretim Etkinliklerinin, Öğrencilerin Bilişsel Tutumlarının Kalıcılığına Olan Etkisinin İncelenmesi," Eğitim Fakültesi Dergisi, Vol. XVIII, No. 2, 2005, pp. 363–382.

Demirel, D. "Etkin Devletin Bir Aracı Olarak e-Devlet ve Türk Kamu Yönetimi," Yayımlanmamış Yüksek Lisans Tezi. Kocaeli Üniversitesi Sosyal Bilimler Enstitüsü, 2005.

Dennis Everette E. "Out of Sight and Out of Mind: The Media Literacy Needs of Grown-Ups," American Behavioral Scientist, Vol. 48, No. 2, 2004, pp. 202–211.

Derry Jan. "Epistemology and Conceptual Resources for the Development of Learning Technologies," Journal of Computer Assisted Learning, Vol. 23, 2007, pp. 503–510.

Deveci Handan, Ruhan Karadağ ve Fatih Yılmaz. "İlköğretim Öğrencilerinin Şiddet Algıları," Elektronik Sosyal Bilimler Dergisi, Vol. 7, No. 24, 2008, pp. 351–368.

Deveci Handan ve Tuba Çengelci. "Sosyal Bilgiler Öğretmen Adaylarından Medya Okuryazarlığına Bir Bakış," Yüzüncü Yıl Üniversitesi Eğitim Fakültesi Dergisi, Vol. V, No. II, 2008, pp. 25–43.

Dönmez, A. "Social Psychology," İmge Press, Ankara, 2003.

Dreßing Harald, Josef Bailer, Anne Anders, Henriette Wagner ve Christine Gallas. "Cyberstalking in a Large Sample of Social Network Users: Prevalance, Characteristics and Impact Upon Victims," Cyberpsychology, Behavior and Social Networking, Vol. 17, No. 2, 2014, pp. 61–67.

Durmuş, Beril ve diğerleri. "Sosyal Bilimlerde SPSS' le Veri Analizi," 4. Baskı, Beta Yayıncılık, İstanbul, 2011.

Erdal, Y. S., & Erdal, Ö. D. "Organized violence in Anatolia: A retrospective research on the injuries from the Neolithic to Early Bronze Age," International Journal of Paleopathology, Vol. 2, No.2–3, 2012, pp. 78–92.

Erjem, Y., & Çağlayandereli, M. "Televizyon ve gençlik: Yerli dizilerin gençlerin model alma davranişi üzerindeki etkisi," CÜ Sosyal Bilimler Dergisi, Vol. 30, No. 1, 2006, pp. 15–30.

Fan M., Huang Y., Qalati S.A., Shah S.M.M., Ostic D. ve Pu Z. "Effects of Information Overload, Communication Overload, and Inequality on Digital Distrust: A Cyber-Violence Behavior Mechanism," Frontiers in Psychology, Vol. 12, 2021, Art. 643981. https://doi.org/10.3389/fpsyg.2021.643981

Ferguson Christopher J. ve Dominic Dyck. "Paradigm Change in Aggression Research: The Time Has Come to Retire the General Aggression Model," Aggression and Violent Behavior, Vol. 17, 2012, pp. 220–228.

Flanagin Andrew J. ve Miriam J. Metzger. "Digital Media and Youth: Unparalleled Opportunity and Unprecedented Responsibility." In Miriam J. Metzger ve Andrew J. Flanagin (Eds.) Digital Media, Youth and Credibility. The John D. and Catherine T. MacArthur Foundation Series on Digital Media and Learning. Cambridge, MA: The MIT Press, 2008, pp. 5–28.

Fox Jesse ve Megan A. Vandemia. "Selective Self-Presentation and Social Comparison Through Photographs on Social Networking Sites," Cyberpsychology, Behavior and Social Networking, Vol. 19, No. 10, 2016, pp. 593–600.

Funk Jeanne B., Heidi Bechtoldt Baldacci, Tracie Pasold ve Jennifer Baumgardner. "Violence Exposure in Real-Life, Video Games, Television, Movies and Internet: Is There Desensitization?," Journal of Adolescence, Vol. 27, 2004, pp. 23–39.

Funk, S., Kellner, D., & Share, J. "Critical media literacy as transformative pedagogy," In Handbook of research on media literacy in the digital age, igi Global, 2016, pp. 1–30.

Gans, H. J. "The American news media in an increasingly unequal society," International Journal of Communication, Vol. 8, 2014, pp. 12.

George, C. "Contentious journalism and the Internet: Towards democratic discourse in Malaysia and Singapore," NUS Press, 2006.

Gencer Zekiye Tamer. "Medyanın Gündem Oluşturma Sürecinde Sosyal Entropinin Rolü Üzerine Uygulamalı Bir Çalışma," Yayınlanmamış Doktora Lisans Tezi. Selçuk Üniversitesi Sosyal Bilimler Enstitüsü, 2012.

Giddens, A. Anthony Giddens. "FIFTY KEY THINKERS IN INTERNATIONAL RELATIONS," SECOND EDITION, 2008, pp. 353.

Gong Jie, Xinguang Chen, Jing Zeng, Fang Li, Dunjin Zhou ve Zengzhen Wang, Z. "Adolescent Addictive Internet Use and Drug Abuse in Wuhan, China," Addiction Research & Theory, Vol. 17, No. 3, 2009, pp. 291–305.

Goodova Margarita, Elena Rubtsova, Rafael Filiberto Forteza Fernandez. "Multimedia Resources as Examples of Polymorphic Educational Hypertexts in the Post-Literacy Era," Procedia, Social and Behavioral Sciences, Vol. 214, 2015, pp. 952–957.

Gökçearslan Şahin ve Mustafa Serkan Günbatar. "Ortaöğrenim Öğrencilerinde İnternet Bağımlılığı," Eğitim Teknolojisi Kuram ve Uygulama Dergisi, Vol. 2, No. 2, 2012, pp. 10–24.

Göker Göksel, Mustafa Demir ve Adem Doğan. "Ağ Toplumunda Sosyalleşme ve Paylaşım: Facebook Üzerine Ampirik Bir Araştırma," e-Journal of New World Sciences Academy, Vol. 5, No. 2, 2010, pp. 183–206.

Gvirsman Shira Dvir, L. Rowell Huesmann, Eric F. Dubow, Simha F. Landau, Paul Boxer ve Khalil Shikaki. "The Longitudinal Effects of Chronic Mediated Exposure to Political Violence on Ideological Beliefs About Political Conflicts Among Youths," Political Communication, Vol. 33, 2016, pp. 98–117.

Guo Xiuyan, Li Zheng, Hongyi Wang, Lei Zhu, Jianqi Li, Qianfeng Wang, Zoltan Dienes ve Zhiliang Yang. "Exposure to Violence Reduces Emphathetic Responses to Other's Pain," Brain and Cognition, Vol. 82, 2013, pp. 187–191.

Gül Songül Sallan ve Yonca Altındal. "Medyada Kadın Cinayeti Haberlerindeki Cinsiyetçi İzler: Radikal Gazetesi," Akdeniz İletişim Dergisi, 2015, pp. 168–188.

Gürel, E., & Yakın, M. "Sözlük sourtimes: Postmodern Electronic Culture," Selçuk Communication, Vol. 4, No. 4, 2007, pp. 203–219.

Güven Selahattin. Medyada Çocuk ve Toplumsal Dönüşüm. Ankara: Orient Yayınları, 2015.

Hargrave, A. M. "How children interpret screen violence," London: British Broadcasting Corporation, 2003.

Hawdon, J., Oksanen, A., & Räsänen, P. "Online extremism and online hate: Exposure among Adolescents and Young Adults in Four Nations," NORDICOM, Vol. 3, 2015, pp. 29–37.

Helfgott Jacqueline B. "Criminal Behavior and the Copyycat Effect: Literature Review and Theoretical Framework for Empirical Investigation," Aggression and Violent Behavior, Vol. 22, 2015, pp. 46–64.

Hinduja Sameer ve Justin W. Patchin. "Bullying, Cyberbullying and Suicide," Archives of Suicide Research, Vol. 14, 2010, pp. 206–221.

Hobbs Renee. Digital and Media Literacy: A Plan of Action, The Aspen Institute Communications and Society Program. Washington, DC: The Aspen Institute, 2010.

Huesmann L. Rowell. "The Impact of Electronic Violence: Scientific Theory and Research," Journal of Adolescent Health, Vol. 41, 2007, pp. S6–S13.

Hummer Tom A., William G. Kronenberger, Yang Wang, Caitlin C. Anderson ve Vincent P. Mathews. "Association of Television Violence Exposure with Executive Functioning and White Matter Volume in Young Adult Males," Brain and Cognition, Vol. 88, 2014, pp. 26–34.

İnceoğlu, Y., & Akıner, N. "Medya ve Çocuk Rehberi: İletişim Araştırmaları İçin Rehber Kitap," Eğitim Press, Konya, 2008.

İnceoğlu, Y. & Çoban, S. "Azınlıklar, Ötekiler ve Medya," Ayrıntı Press, İstanbul, 2015.

İnci Ülkü H. "Basında Yer Alan Namus Cinayetlerinin Sosyolojik Analizi," Tarih Kültür ve Sanat Araştırmaları Dergisi, Vol. 2, No. 3, 2013, pp. 282–296.

Jenkins Henry ve Mark Deuze. "Convergence Culture" Convergence: The International Journal of Research into New Media Technologies, Vol. 14, No. 1, 2008, pp. 5–12.

Jenson, J., & Lewis, L. A. "The adoring audience: Fan culture and popular media," The Adoring Audience: Fan Culture and Popular Media, 1992, pp. 9–29.

Jones Christopher ve Laura Czerniewicz. "Describing or Debunking? The Net Generation and Gigital Natives," Journal of Computer Assisted Learning, Vol. 26, 2010, pp. 317–320.

Jost John T. ve Orsolya Hunyady. "The Psychology of System Justification and Palliative Function of Ideology," Europian Review of Social Psychology, Vol. 13, 2002, pp. 111–153.

Juvonen Jaana ve Elisheva F. Gross. "Extending the School Grounds?—Bullying Experiences in Cyberspace," Journal of School Health, Vol. 78, No. 9, 2008, pp. 496–505.

Kalan Özlem Gündüz. "Medya Okuryazarlığı ve Okul Öncesi Çocuk: Ebeveynlerin Medya Okuryazarlığı Bilinci Üzerine Bir Araştırma," İletişim Fakültesi Dergisi, 2010, pp. 59–73.

Kafai Yasmin B. ve Kylie A. Peppler. "Youth, Technology and DIY: Developing Participatory Competencies in Creative Media Production," Review of Research in Education, Vol. 35, 2011, pp. 89–119.

Kalnin Andrew J., Chad R. Edwards, Yang Wang, William G. Kronenberger, Tom A. Hummer, Kristine M. Mosier, David W. Dunn ve Vincent P. Mathews. "The Interacting Role of Media Violence Exposure and Aggressive—Disruptive Behavior in Adolescent Brain Activation During an Emotional Stroop Task," Psychiatry Research: Neuroimaging, Vol. 192, 2011, pp. 12–19.

Kara Taylan. "Görsel Medyanın Aile Bireyleri Üzerindeki Etkisi Üzerine Bir Araştırma," Yayımlanmamış TUİK Uzmanlık Tezi, TUİK, 2011.

Karagülle Ayşegül Elif ve Berk Çaycı. "Ağ Toplumunda Sosyalleşme ve Yabancılaşma," The Turkish Online Journal of Design, Art and Communication, Vol. 4, No. 1, 2014, pp. 1–9.

Kartal Osman Yılmaz ve Remzi Y. Kıncal. "Medya Okuryazarlığı Eğitimi Alan Rehberlik ve Psikolojik Danışmanlık Anabilim Dalı Öğrencilerinin Aktif Vatandaşlık Düzeylerini Etkileyen Faktörler," M.Ü. Atatürk Eğitim Fakültesi Eğitim Bilimleri Dergisi, Vol. 36, 2012, pp. 169–191.

Kellij, S., Lodder, G.M.A., van den Bedem, N. et al. "The Social Cognitions of Victims of Bullying: A Systematic Review", Adolescent Research Review, Vol. 7, 2022, pp. 287–334. https://doi.org/10.1007/s40894-022-00183-8

Kelly Christopher R., Jack Grinband ve Joy Hirsch. "Repeated Exposure to Media Violence is Associated with Diminished Response in an Inhibitory Frontolimbic Network," PLoS ONE, Vol. 12, e1268, 2007, pp. 1–8.

Kevorkian Melanie M. ve Robin D'antona. 101 Facts About Bullying: What Everyone Should Know. Rowmann & Littlefield Education, 2008.

Kiewitz Christian ve James B. Weaver. "Trait Aggressiveness, Media Violence and Perceptions of Interpersonal Conflict," Personality and Individual Differences, Vol. 31, No. 6, 2001, pp. 821–835.

Koçer, Birsen. "Saldırganlık ve Video Oyunları: Şiddetin Meşruluğunun ve Stereotipik Hedefin Etkisi," Yayımlanmamış Yüksek Lisans Tezi. ODTÜ Sosyal Bilimler Enstitüsü, 2015.

Kowalski, R. M., & Limber, S. P. "Electronic bullying among middle school students," Journal of adolescent health, Vol. 41, No. 6, 2007, pp. 22–30.

Köknel, Ö. "Bireysel ve Toplumsal Şiddet," Altın Kitaplar Press, İstanbul, 2000.

Krcmar, M., & Valkenburg, P. M. "A scale to assess children's moral interpretations of justified and unjustified violence and its relationship to television viewing," Communication Research, Vol. 26, No.5, 1999, pp. 608–634.

Kurt Adile Aşkım ve Dilruba Kürüm, D. "Medya Okuryazarlığı ve Eleştirel Düşünme Arasındaki İlişki: Kavramsal Bir Bakış," Mehmet Akif Ersoy Üniversitesi Sosyal Bilimler Enstitüsü Dergisi, Vol. 2, No. 2, 2010, pp. 20–34.

Langos Colette. "Cyberbullying: The Challenge to Define," Cyberpsychology, Behavior and Social Networking, Vol. 15, No. 6, 2012, pp. 285–289.

Lawrence R.A.A.R. "The Influence of Media on the Incidence of Violence," Journal of Clinical Forensic Medicine, Vol. 4, 1997, pp. 163–165.

Lear Tom van. "The Means of Justify the End: Comabting Cyber Harassment in Social Media," Journal of Business Ethics, Vol. 123, 2014, pp. 85–98.

Li, C. K., Holt, T. J., Bossler, A. M., & May, D. C. "Examining the mediating effects of social learning on the low self-control—Cyberbullying relationship in a youth sample," Deviant Behavior, Vol. 37, No. 2, 2016, pp. 126–138.

Li, Q. "Bullying in the new playground: Research into cyberbullying and cyber victimisation," Australasian Journal of Educational Technology, Vol. 23, No. 4, 2007.

Li Qing. "Cyberbullying in High Schools: A Study of Students's Behaviors and Beliefs About This New Phenomenon," Journal of Aggression, Maltreatment & Trauma, Vol. 19, 2010, pp. 371–392.

Literat Ioana. "Measuring New Media Literacies: Towards the Development of a Comprehensive Assessment Tool," Journal of Media Literacy Education, Vol. 6, No. 1, 2014, pp. 15–27.

Livingstone Sonia. "Media Literacy and the Challenge of New Information and Communication Technologies," The Communication Review, Vol. 7, No. 1, 2004, pp. 3–14.

Lv, Y. "Cultivation of Teenagers' Digital Media Literacy and Network Legal Literacy in the Era of Digital Virtual Technology," Hindawi Scientific Programming, Vol. 2022, Art. 2978460, 2022, pp. 1–9. https://doi.org/10.1155/2022/2978460

Madianu Mirca ve Daniel Miller. "Polymedia: Towards a New Theory of Digital Media in Interpersonal Communication," International Journal of Cultural Studies, Vol. 16, No. 2, 2012, pp. 169–187.

Mason Kimberly L. "Cyberbullying: A Preliminary Assessment for School Personnel", Psychology in the Schools, Vol. 45, No. 4, pp. 323–348.

Meller Robert H. "The Effects of Television Violence on Children," Current Pediatrics, Vol. 6, 1996, pp. 2017–220.

Merwe P. van Der. "Adolescent Violence: The Risks and Benefits of Electronic Media Technology," Procedia-Social and Behavioral Sciences, Vol. 82, 2013, pp. 87–93.

McKenna, K. Y., & Bargh, J. A. "Plan 9 from cyberspace: The implications of the Internet for personality and social psychology," Personality and social psychology review, Vol. 4, No. 1, 2000, pp. 57–75.

Molen, Juliette H. Walma van der ve Brad J. Bushman. "Children's Direct Fright and Worry Reactions to Violence in Fiction and News Television Programs," Journal of Pediatrics, September 2008, pp. 420–424.

Morgan, Michael ve James Shanahan. "The State of Cultivation," Journal of Broadcasting & Electronic Media, Vol. 54, No. 2, pp. 337–355.

Moses, Rafeal. "Şiddet Nerede Başlıyor?," Cogito, Vol. 6–7, 1996, pp. 23–28.

Mountford Victoria A., Kate Tchanturia ve Lucia Valmaggia. " 'What Are You Thinking When You Look at Me?' A Pilot Study of the Use of Virtual Reality in Body Image," Cyberpsychology, Behavior and Social Networking, Vol. 19, No. 2, 2016, pp. 93–99.

Mrah, I. "Digital Media Literacy in the Age of Mis/Disinformation: The Case of Moroccan University Students," Digital Education Review, Vol. 41, 2022, pp. 176–194.

Nar Mehmet Şükrü. "The Effect of Media as a Tool of Popular Culture on Crime," Journal of Studies in Social Sciences, Vol. 9, No. 1, 2014, pp. 1–21.

Narmanlıoğlu Haldun. "Televizyon İmajı ve Sosyal Gerçeklik," Turkish Studies, International Periodical for the Languages, Literature and History of Turkish or Turkic, Vol. 11, No. 2, 2016, pp. 935–950.

Natharrius David. "The More We Know, the More We See: The Role of Visuality in Media Literacy," American Behavioral Scientist, Vol. 48, No. 2, 2004, pp. 238–247.

Oliver Martin. "Technological Determinism in Educational Technology Research: Some Alternative Ways of Thinking About the Relationship Between Learning and Technology," Journal of Computer Assisted Learning, Vol. 27, 2011, pp. 373–384.

Ögel, K. "Internet Bağımlılığı: Internetin Psikolojisini Anlamak ve Bağımlılıkla Başa Çıkmak," İş Bankası Press, İstanbul, 2012.

Önk, Ü. Y., & Selçuk, S. S. "Ekrandaki "Öteki": 2000 Sonrası Yerli Dizilerde Azınlıkların Temsili," Journal of Culture and Communication, Vol.1, No. 7, 2014, pp. 2.

Pabian, S., & Vandebosch, H. "An investigation of short-term longitudinal associations between social anxiety and victimization and perpetration of traditional bullying and cyberbullying," Journal of youth and adolescence, Vol. 45, 2016, pp. 328–339.

Park Sora. "Dimensions of Digital Media Literacy and the Relationship with Social Exclusion," Media International Australia, Vol. 142, 2012, pp. 87–100.

Parrott Dominic J. "A Theoretical Framework for Antigay Aggression: Review of Established and Hypothesized Effects within the Context of the General Aggression Model," Clinical Psychology Review, Vol. 28, 2008, pp. 933–951.

Pennell Amanda E. ve Kevin D. Browne. "Film Violence and Young Offenders," Aggression and Violent Behavior, Vol. 4, No. 1, 1999, pp. 13–28.

Pişkin Günseli. "Günümüzde Türkiye'de Sinema Filmleriyle Televizyon Dizilerinde Kadınlar ve Töre," Doğu Anadolu Bölgesi Araştırmaları, Vol. 6, No. 2, 2008, pp. 39–46.

Read Glenna L., Mary Ballard, Lisa J. Emery ve Doris G. Bazzini. "Examining Desensitization Usial Facial Electromyography: Violent Videogames, Gender and Affective Responding," Computer in Human Behavior, Vol. 62, 2016, pp. 201–211.

Satan, A. "Ergenlerde akran baskısı benlik saygısı ve alkol kullanımı arasındaki ilişkilerin incelenmesi," Marmara University Atatürk Education Faculty Journal of Educational Science, Vol. 34, No. 34, 2011, pp. 183–194.

Savrun Mert. Biyolojik, Sosyolojik, Psikolojik Açıdan Şiddet. İstanbul: Yüce Yayım, 2000, 140 p.

Selkie Ellen M., Rajitha Kota, Ya-Fen Chan ve Megan Moreno. "Cyberbullying, Depression and Problem Alcohol Use in Female College Students: A Multisite Study," Cyberpsychology, Behavior and Social Networking, (2015) Vol. 18, No. 2, pp. 79–86.

Sparks, G. G., Sparks, C. W., & Sparks, E. A. "Media violence," In Media effects, Routledge, 2009, pp. 285–302.

Steinerman Joshua R., Richard B. Lipton, Bruce D. Rapkin, Brian R. Quaranto ve Carolyn E. Schwartz. "Factors Associated with Openess to Research Participation in an Aging Community: The Importance of Technophilia and Social Cohesion," Technophilia, Vol. 11, No. 4, 2013, pp. 504–512.

Stephens, A. N., Trawley, S. L., & Ohtsuka, K. "Venting anger in cyberspace: Self-entitlement versus self-preservation in# roadrage tweets," Transportation research part F: traffic psychology and behaviour, Vol. 42, 2016, pp. 400–410.

Subrahmanyam Kaveri ve Patricia Greenfield. "Online Communication and Adolescents Relationships," The Future of Children, Vol. 18, No. 1, 2008, pp. 121–146.

Sucu İpek. "Sosyal Medya Oyunlarında Gerçeklik Olgusunun Yön Değiştirmesi: Smeet Oyunu Örneği," Gümüşhane Üniversitesi İletişim Fakültesi Elektronik Dergisi, Vol. 3, 2012, pp. 55–88.

Suler, J. "The online disinhibition effect," Cyberpsychology & Behavior, Vol.7, No. 3, 2004, pp. 321–326.

Suwana, F. "Content, Changers, Community and Collaboration: Expanding Digital Media Literacy Initiatives," Media Practice and Education, Vol. 22, No. 2, 2021, pp. 153–170 https://doi.org/10.1080/25741136.2021.1888192

Şeker Tülin ve Fadime Şimşek, F. "Kodlama—Kodaçımı Bağlamında Muhteşem Yüzyıl Dizisinin Lise Öğrencileri Üzerindeki Etkilerine Yönelik Alımlama Analizi," Selçuk İletişim, Vol. 7, No. 2, 2012, pp. 111–120.

Şener, N. K. "Eğlencenin gözetleme hâli ya da eğlence endüstrisinde "görünen" ve "gören" olmak," TRT Akademi Press, Entertainment Volume, Vol. 1, No.1, 2016, pp. 50–70.

Teenage Research Unlimited. "Tech abuse in teenrelationships study," Teenage Research Unlimited, Inc., Northbrook, IL, 2007

Teyfur, M. "Basında Yer Alan Okullarda Şiddet ile İlgili Olayların Değerlendirilmesi," İlköğretim Online, Vol. 13, No. 4, 2014, pp. 1311–1330.

Toker Huriye ve Derya Altun, D. "Toplumsal Şiddetin Aktarım Yoluyla Yeniden Üretilmesi: Basının Televizyonlaşması Bağlamında Şefika Etik Cinayeti," Selçuk İletişim Dergisi, Vol. 9, No. 1, 2015, pp. 115–140.

Tutar, H. "Social Psychology," Seçkin Press, İstanbul, 2012.

118 REFERENCES

Ulaş, A. H., Epçaçan, C., & Koçak, B. "The concept of "Media Literacy" and an evaluation on the necessity of media literacy education in creating awareness towards Turkish language," Procedia-Social and Behavioral Sciences, Vol. 31, 2012, pp. 376–382.

Valenzuela Sebastián, Daniel Halpern ve James E. Katz. "Social Network Sites, Marriage Well-Being and Divorce: Survey and State-Level Evidence from the United States," Computers in Human Behavior, Vol. 36, 2014, pp. 94–101.

Varnhagen, C. K. "Children and the Internet," In Psychology and the Internet, Academic Press, 2007, pp. 37–54..

Velotti Patrizia, Carlo Garofalo, Chiara Petrocchi, Francesca Cavallo, Raffaele Popolo ve Giancarlo Dimaggio. "Alexithymia, Emotional Dysregulation, Impulsivity and Aggression: A Multiple Mediation Model," Psychiatry Research, Vol. 237, 2016, pp. 296–303.

Westley, W. A. "Violence and the police," American Journal of Sociology, Vol. 59, No.1, 1953, pp. 34–41.

Wiedeman, Ashlee M., Jacqueline A. Black, Autumn L. Dolle, Emmanuel J. Finney ve Kendell L. Coker. "Factors Influencing the Impact og Aggressive and Violent Media on Children and Adolescents," Aggression and Violent Behavior, Vol. 25, 2015, pp. 191–198.

Wong, R. Y. M., Cheung, C. M., Xiao, B., ve Thatcher, J. B. "Standing up or standing by: Understanding Bystanders' Proactive Reporting Responses to Social Media Harassment", Information Systems Research, Vol. 32, No. 2, 2021, pp. 561–581.

Yardi, Sarita ve Danah Boyd. "Dynamic Debates: An Analysis of Group Polarization Over Time on Twitter," Bulletin of Science, Technology & Society, Vol. 30, No. 5, 2010, pp. 316–327.

Yazıcı, M. "The Relationship Between Social Change With Form Of Violence: Usa / Europe - Turkey Comparison," Electronic Journal of Social Sciences, Vol. 12, No. 46, 2013, pp. 350–369.

Ybarra, M. L., & Mitchell, K. J. "Exposure to Internet pornography among children and adolescents: A national survey," Cyberpsychology & behavior, Vol. 8, No. 5, 2005, pp. 473–486.

Ybarra, L. Michele, Danah Boyd, Josephine D. Korchmaros ve Jay Koby Oppenheim. "Defining and Measuring Cyberbullying Within the Larger Context of Bullying Victimization," Journal of Adolescent Health, Vol. 51, 2012, pp. 53–58.

Yeğen, Ceren. "Bir Dijital Aktivizm Biçimi Olarak Slaktivizm: Change.Org Örneği," Karadeniz Teknik Üniversitesi (KTÜ) İletişim Araştırmaları Dergisi, Vol. 5, No. 8, 2015, pp. 84–108.

Yeğen, Ceren. "Çocuk Cinayet Haberlerinin Türk Yazılı Basınında Sunumu: Posta Gazetesi Örneği," Global Media Journal TR Edition, Vol. 5, No. 10, 2015, pp. 363-384.

Yılmaz, Berkant, Dündar, Güher ve Oskay, Taala. "Dijital Ortamda Aktivizm: Online İmza Kampanyalarına Katılım Davranışlarının İncelenmesi", E-Journal of Intermedia, Vol. 2, No. 2, 2015, pp. 481-504.

Zimmermann, B. "Pragmatism and the capability approach: Challenges in social theory and empirical research," European Journal of Social Theory, Vol. 9, No. 4, 2006, pp. 467-484.

Zorlu, Yaşar. "Medyadaki Şiddet ve Etkileri," Humanities Sciences, Vol. 11, No. 1, 2016, pp. 13-32.

Borrajo, E., Gamez-Guadix, M. ve Calvete, E. "Justification Beliefs of Violence, Myths about Love and Cyber Dating Abuse," Psicothema, Vol. 27, No. 4, 2015, pp. 327-333.

Calvete, E. "Justification of Violence and Grandiosity Schemas as Predictors of Antisocial Behavior in Adolescents," Journal of Abnormal Child Psychology, Vol. 36, 2008, pp. 1083-1095.

Chetty, N. ve Alathur, S. "Hate Speech Review in the Context of Online Social Networks," Agression and Violent Behavior, Vol. 40, 2018, pp. 108-118.

Dodge, K.A. ve Rabiner, D.L. "Returning to Roots: On Social Information Processing and Moral Development," Child Development, Vol. 75, No. 4, 2004, 1003-1008.

Haroon, M., Chhabra, A., Liu, X., Mohapatra, P., Shafiq, Z. ve Wojcieszak, M. "YouTube, The Great Radicalizer? Auding and Mitigating Ideological Biases in YouTube Recommendations," 2022, https://arxiv.org/abs/2203.10666

Harris, A. ve Johns, A. "Youth, Social Cohesion and Digital Life: From Risk and Resilience to a Global Citizenship Approach," Journal of Sociology, Vol. 57, 2020, pp. 394-411.

Hawdon, J., Oksanen, A. ve Rasanen, P. "Online Extremism and Online Hate: Exposure Among Adolescents and Young Adults Four Nations," Nordicom-Information, Vol. 37, No. 3(4), 2015, pp. 29-37.

Gerstenfeld, Phyllis B., Diana R. Grant, ve Chau-Pu Chiang. "Hate Online: A Content Analysis of Extremist Internet Sites," Analyses of Social Issues and Public Policy, Vol. 3, No. 1, 2003, pp. 29-44.

Linares, R., Aranda, M., Garcia-Domingo, M., Amezcua, T., Fuentes, V. ve Moreno-Padilla, M. "Cyber-dating Abuse in Young Adult Couples: Relations with Sexist Attitudes and Violence Justification, Smartphone Usage and Impulsivity," PLoS ONE, Vol. 16, No. 6, 2021, Art. e0253180.

Malle, B. F. "Moral Judgments," Annual Review of Psychology, Vol. 72, No. 1, 2021, 293–318.

McCauley, Clark, ve Sophia Moskalenko. "Mechanisms of Political Radicalization: Pathways toward Terrorism", Terrorism and Political Violence, Vol. 20, No. 3, 2008, pp. 415–433.

Pinciotti, C. M., ve Orcutt, H. K. "Understanding Gender Differences in Rape Victim Blaming: The Power of Social Influence and Just World Beliefs," Journal of Interpersonal Violence, Vol. 36, No. 1–2, 2021, pp. 255–275.

Polonska-Kimunguyi, E. "War, Resistance and Refuge: Racism and double standards in western media coverage of Ukraine [Blog]," LSE, 2022.

Tekoniemi, S., Kotilainen, S., Maasilta, M., ve Lempiäinen, K. "Fact-Checking as Digital Media Literacy in Higher Education", Seminar.Net, Vol. 18, No. 1, 2022. https://doi.org/10.7577/seminar.4689

Wang, C., Platow, M. J., Bar-Tal, D., Augoustinos, M., Van Rooy, D., ve Spears, R. "When Are Intergroup Attitudes Judged as Free Speech and When as Prejudice? A Social Identity Analysis of Attitudes towards Immigrants," International Journal of Psychology, Vol. 57, No. 4, 2022, pp. 456–465.

Wang, J., Wang, Z., Liu, X., Yang, X., Zheng, M., ve Bai, X. "The Impacts of a COVID-19 Epidemic Focus and General Belief in a Just World on Individual Emotions," Personality and Individual Differences, Vol. 168, 2021, Art. 110349.

Weimann, Gabriel. "Virtual Disputes: The Use of the Internet for Terrorist Debates," Studies in Conflict and Terrorism, Vol. 29, No. 7, 2006, 623–639.

Winter, C., Neumann, P., Meleagrou-Hitchens, A., Ranstorp, M., Vidino, L., ve Fürst, J. "Online Extremism: Research Trends in Internet Activism, Radicalization, and Counterstrategies," International Journal of Conflict and Violence, Vol. 14, No. 2, 2020, pp. 1–20. https://doi.org/10.4119/ijcv-3809

Zeng, P., Zhao, X., Xie, X., Long, J., Jiamg, Q., Wang, Y., Qi, L. ve Lei, L. "Moral Perfectioanism and Online Prosocial Behavior: The Mediating Role of Moral Identity and the Moderating Role of Online Interpersonal Trust," Personality and Individual Differences, Vol. 162, 2020, Art. 110017.

www.ingramcontent.com/pod-product-compliance
Lightning Source LLC
Chambersburg PA
CBHW070350270326
41926CB00017B/4075